IN THE SPRING OF 1979, Jim Krusoe, who programmed readings at Beyond Baroque,* was preparing to leave for a teaching career at SMC. For his "last hurrah" at BB, he scheduled an evening of humorous poetry "at your own risk." The evening's offerings included Michael Silverblatt (now of KCRW) doing something about fairies, Bob Flanagan impersonating celebrities reading local poets' works, and Scott Wannberg reading a "radio play" called CONDOS FROM HELL!

It was, as Scott described it, a sort of "John Agar sci-fi movie" done as an old-time radio play, complete with a commercial for a Classic Book of the Month Club. As I remember the commercial, a mother and father were concerned that after having subscribed to the classic book club, their son, who had read "David Copperfield" through the club, was walking around the house chanting:

"Uriah Heap! Uriah Heap!"

If you knew Scott, you would know how he did the boy's voice chanting Uriah Heap. Would you subscribe to a book of the month club if you heard that radio spot?

On to the actual radio play. Scott did all the voices and sound effects. The Condo from Hell broke loose from its roots in Venice and went on a rampage through Los Angeles. The cops tried to stop it and the National Guard had to be called

---

*Beyond Baroque is the venerable mecca of the Los Angeles poetry community located in Venice, California.

in. The audience could hardly keep up with the opportunities to laugh.

I don't think there was a recording of CONDOS FROM HELL and I don't know if the manuscript exists. Like ancient Greek comedies, which were written to be performed once, Scott's comedy masterpiece was a one-time event and if the script does surface and someone stages it, it will still never be quite what it sounded like that night.

* * *

The second memory is more personal. I was at a post-reading party at someone's house and I was upset. I was infatuated with someone and he wasn't interested in me. I was crying. Scott noticed. He noticed things like that. He passed me a note, In the note, which was a draft of a poem, he asked me and the someone to forgive and like each other.

Later on, Scott introduced a poem at Beyond Baroque, called "Lynne Bronstein's Poem." It was about me. It was about my sad love and my own poetry and how it inspired him. Fortunately, this poem survives. S.A. Griffin included it in the massive Scott Wannberg collection "The Official Language of Yes." S.A. has described the poem as "one of the earliest Scott Wannberg poems." Well, there were even earlier ones but 1978 was a pivotal year, the year that I think Scott became Scott and people started taking notice.

> **Lynne Bronstein**— she is a poet, journalist, fiction writer, and won't give up hoping.

Scott Wannberg was the King of the Kingdom of Yes

and developed the language that spoke directly to
the hearts of thousands of people who normally
did not even read or listen to poetry. His style was one of
an almost inexplicable combination of dancing on paper
and a print verbality that struck the mind in the voice of each reader
and taught them all they needed to know about Yes on that day.

His live performances were legendary and especially,
dressed in one of his very special t-shirts,
he would render his version of John Prine's Sam Stone
that would always leave the listeners stunned.

Some leave the tap running like water is free in this desert,
But, I am SO thirsty for Scott, just Scott, right now;
But he is late, just late for now, not gone.

He was the ringmaster,
The ringleader,
The ring barer,
The Master Baiter
With this big black shiny boots
And that top hat in the center ring
blowing the whistle of YesYes.
I loved that whistle.
You DO know how to whistle, doncha?
You just put your lips together and.....
OK, you can come in and blow now
James Moody, I'm through.....

Hank Beukema— lives, it seems, on Facebook and records his poetic interpretations on YouTube at *https://www.youtube.com/user/buckmaniac* — check him out!

SCOTT WANNBERG
The LUMMOX Years

*Being a collection of Scott's contributions
to the LUMMOX Journal
and LUMMOX Press
between 1996 and 2006*

Edited by RD Armstrong

©2016 RD Armstrong

Writing by Scott Wannberg © Estate of Scott Wannberg, used with permission.

All rights reserved. No part of this book may be reproduced without the express written permission of the author, except in the case of written reviews.

Front Cover illustration by Michael Paul
Back Cover photo by Raindog

ISBN 978-1-9298-7854-3

Library of Congress Control Number: 2016962918

First edition

PO Box 5301
San Pedro, CA 90733
www.lummoxpress.com/lc

Printed in the United States of America

Acknowledgments

We would like to thank all the poets and editors and musicians and songwriters who encouraged Scott who then turned around and gave as good as he got, ten-fold. Also, I'd like to thank the folks in charge of Scott's literary estate, without whom this book might not have ever happened. Finally, I would like to thank Scott for gracing my life in the magic of his; like Bukowski, Scott was a "one-off" – we won't see another like him in our collective lifetimes.

Table of Concepts

ii- Remembrance of Scott BY LYNNE BRONSTEIN
iv- Remembrance of Scott BY HANK BEUKEMA

x- Introduction BY RD ARMSTRONG

The *LUMMOX Journal* Years
- *2-* Ella – *August 1996*
- *3-* Process Rap – *May 1997*
- *5-* An Impression – *August 1997*
- *9-* No Mistakes – *February 1998*
- *11-* transfusion of a soul – *April 1998 (All Poetry Issue)*
- *13-* Just What A National Poetry Month *Might* Mean – *June 1998*
- *17-* Russian Dissident Hootenanny – *August 1998*
- *19-* Reviews by Scott Wannberg – *December 1998*
- *22-* Scott Wannberg Interview – *January 1999*
- *30-* Littleton – *1999*
- *33-* poetry says yes – *September/October 2005*
- *34-* Where the rivers run – *March/April 2006*
- *35-* The Revolution Has Been Remaindered – *March/April 2005*
- *37-* The Dove Has Fangs – *September/October 2004*
- *38-* the possibility of life – *October 2003*
- *40-* send out for a crying room… – *April 2003*
- *42-* John Prine Rap – *June 2002*
- *43-* John Thomas, He Had a Hammer – *May 2002*
- *44-* Border of Boredom – *April 2000*
- *45-* Rambler, American – *February 2000*
- *46-* The Unknown Bukowski Thriller – *August 1999*
- *48-* The road that takes you – *January/February 2004*

49- Earth Fell Hard – *April 2002*

51- In the House of Warren Oates – *October 2002*

53- Reviews – *July 2001*

55- Language from the bottom... – *November 2000*

56- Charles Bukowski, Mountain Man – *August 2000*

60- Review – *December 1999*

61- Rant #1 – *Date unknown*

62- Scarecrow – *January 1999*

66- bucketful of yes – *"All Poetry Issue" April 1999*

The Little Red Book Series

68- **Equal Opportunity Sledgehammer** – *1999*

108- **Nomads of Oblivion** – *2000*

148- from **Eyes Like Mingus** – Ella – *1999*

Special Edition Books

149- from **Last Call** – Bukowski Rap – *2004*

151- **Colorado River Song** – *2001*

156- About Scott Wannberg

157- Bibliography

158- Remembrance BY STEVE GOLDMAN

161- Remembrance BY DONA MARY DIRLAM

162- Remembrance BY VICTOR D. INFANTE

164- Remembrance BY DOUG KNOTT

About this book

I FIRST MET SCOTT WANNBERG in 1994. Charles Bukowski had died and as the dishwashing poet of San Pedro (as I was known back then), it fell to me to hold some sort memorial reading in his honor. The owners of the coffeehouse where I earned my name, Chris and Jeanette Roth, thought it would be a great idea since they knew the Bukowski's to some extent...but that applied to a lot of people who knew them (or thought they did).

    I knew a few poets in the area, but thought that it would be a better idea if we could get a lot more poets and make it a real blow-out! So, I began to rattle some cages. Someone recommended an actor, whose name I've forgotten, who supposedly knew a lot of poets in Los Angeles. I contacted him, got some names and numbers and started reaching out to them. When I got a sympathetic response I asked them to extend the invitation to their contacts, and so the invite spread (this was before "going viral" had been coined, before email was in common use, and before everyone had a cellphone... yes, children, there was a time when we lived without the internet). In time, we had about 30 poets lined up, and I was assured that they were "heavy hitters". And almost everyone who read that night was. Many of my poetry relationships here in the L.A. area, began on that night in April.

    Just to make things more interesting, I also put together a band of musicians I knew locally. To be honest I only knew a couple of them, and only because I had booked them to play at Sacred Grounds (the coffeehouse I mentioned). There was Joe Baiza on guitar, Ralph Gorodetsky on bass, Mike Watt on bass, Stephen Hodges on drums and some guy nicknamed Raindog on a Casio saxophone! In my defense, one, I just didn't know any better and two, I don't really know how to do anything half way (anybody who knows me can tell you that).

So, imagine a band jamming for about an hour and a half on a stage with a steady stream of poets reading their immortal verse to a packed house and you might get a sense of what this night was like. It was electric (I have it on tape)!

Out of this swirling cauldron of creativity and/or chaos came a man, a big man...musta weighed 240, six-three or four with an impish smile and a twinkle in his eye; he stepped up to the mic and delivered his poem or riff or whatever it was and we all loved him!

That man was Scott Wannberg.

Through the years, our paths continued to cross. He worked at a bookstore on the west side called Dutton's and whenever I was up that way I'd stop in and hang out. He was a fountain of info, on music, on movies...he even introduced me to the work of Dennis LeHane. He loved to riff on the language. He was a natural and I believe that if he'd played, he would have been the king of Scat. I remember the first time I heard him read Ella, his iconic poem about Ella Fitzgerald, the phrasing of the words was very similar to a Mingus bass-line. The line, half-remembered some 20 years ago, had something to do with things that happened when "Ella Fitzgerald sang... oxygen was invented, the sun on it's way to the bank had to stop and bop up and down to the music..." It's hard to describe but I can hear Scott's voice working with the syllables and the spaces between them, between the silences and the notes. Magical.

This collection of poems, riffs and ramblings concerns itself with Scott's participation in the *LUMMOX Journal* from 1996 to 2006...almost the entire time that I published the little monthly! It also includes the two Little Red Books that I published for him, **Equal Opportunity Sledgehammer** and **Nomads of Oblivion**, which actually made it onto the Los Angeles Times Top Ten Book list in October 1999! Nomads of Oblivion sold over 400 copies in a month...that's how much he was loved!

I wanted to publish this collection of Scott's work to bring it to a wider audience *and* be entered into the American canon of literature. Though his work was peppered with metaphor, the message always comes through. Whether he's talking about a little girl raped and murdered in a casino bathroom, or a young man bludgeoned to death in Wyoming because he was gay, or the power of Ella Fitzgerald's voice, his words were true and free from moralizing. I think this was the real power of his work. I hope that the reader enjoys this cross-section of Scott's work as it appeared in my old *LUMMOX Journal* (not to be confused with the LUMMOX Poetry Anthology that I have been publishing annually since 2012). I wish he were alive today if for no other reason than to hear him read some of my favorite poems. I hope you will agree with me after you have read this book, that he was one helluva writer! Scott was special. I can't emphasize that enough. He was magic.

RD Armstrong
Long Beach, CA

The
LUMMOX JOURNAL
Years

Ella – *August 1996*

ella fitzgerald sang
oxygen got discovered
the sun, on its way to the bank to the bank to make a deposit
just sort of had to hang there a minute
bopping down and up to the tune
of ella's singing
ella fitzgerald sang
cities rose up from dirt
the buildings of them had people
inside them and
inside those people there were
stories and bloodstreams
that were the songs ella
fitzgerald sang
the sun really had to make it to the bank
before it closed
otherwise it would be overdrawn
and when the sun gets overdrawn
we all get burned
ella fitzgerald sang
armies threw down their guns
the time for dying
had not come to just yet
the sun hovered there
not wanting to go
ella fitzgerald sang
and the stories in her songs
are the stories that keep
us from going under

This poem also appears in the Little Red Book, **Eyes Like Mingus** *LRB#8.*

the last page
Process Rap – *May 1997*

The process just called me collect. I wish it could afford its own phonebill. I think I might have told you about it once, the process. Sleek and sensual, somehow vulnerable, in the weather that never ends. Sometimes you try to disown the thing, throw it out the open window, but it bounces back regardless. Some kind of ongoing voodoo attached to its ability to stick to you, even when you try and change all the shoes in the world you ever thought you owned. The process almost got the lead in some international epic but the money all burned up right before the cameras were set to hum. The process got nominated for some specious thing and it had to go and rent a tux in order to make it to the hootenanny.

We were singing all the songs we never knew all that well. Back there in the room of enduring. The one with the walls that feel good when you know you just can't go on. Process takes your daughter on a date. Don't trust it, now. Look in the big book of phones under the page of yellow and see under process, what it just might warn you. The relatives of time disappear and when they show up again for the reunion they have odd ways of looking you up and down and saying, yeah, I think I know you, cousin.

Make it to the hootenanny is the title of the process' soon to be released tell all autobiography. I'd like to share a bit from the galley I found at my door one cold morning. Listen to the process talk. . .

Process: (234 of Make It To The Hootenanny)

I have no parents. I have no brain. I just take up the magic and when the fires erupt you have no choice but to bathe in my tissue.

I hear the cattle sing a rich Gaelic. I hear the El trains of love whisper above my neck. I am your guardian angel worst nightmare, I'm the deck of the last ship in the world on its way down for the final act of some play you thought you wrote years ago when your faculties could figure things.

(so ends the excerpt. Soon to be a major motion picture no doubt.)

The jukebox knows all your secrets, love. Sit down now on the couch and sing your latest. The afternoon has a headache and the pioneers swear they are unable to continue on. The hit parade just claimed it wrote everything you think you know. We stumble around the rubble of our thought process and now and then a lucid bird sits on a frayed wire and sings a tune that kinetically embraces you.

Process drives up in a sleek stolen limo. Process is on a first name basis with Billy Bob Thornton. Process has its own mid-season replacement series on one of the major networks.

Process is finally who we are when we can't be anything else. Go on, open the door, it's out there, with your name on it. Take it on in and see where the whirlwind rides.

Until the next roundup, this has been your weather report helicopter bouncing up and down and even now and then a bit sideways. We now return you to our sponsored program of the decade . . .

An Impression – *August 1997*

I come back to Bukowski, I go to that room, knowing the stories there are always the kind I can run along with. The language he wielded, or welded, was never obtuse or so archly lofty that I would get buried in it.

I can't even tell you if I rate as a poet or not. I seemingly am unable at composing pristine tiny jewels of enriching language. I can sort of put something together out of prose noises, I guess, and somebody once accused me of writing prose and not poetry, and I said I guess you might be right, maybe they are short short stories passing as poetry, but then again they just might be poems.

There is a difference between poems and poetry. Poetry is John Keats or William Shakespeare. Phrases that you can memorize and throw out at parties and dazzle the body politic with.

Poems, on the other hand, are energy bursts in stanzaic form (and the stanzas do find their own life) you might not be able to memorize and throw out at people at the tip of a hat, but are things you come back to in your own time and rhythm.

Bukowski opened the skylight for me and let the air in. He showed me you could write in the syntax you saw and heard in. You didn't need to elaborate and hang the special ornament at the top of the tree. Tinsel would get you home, even tinsel that had been kind of dog-eared in the box from lack of use.

In Taylor Hackford's documentary about Bukowski, the man pointed to his typewriter (it was before the computer—he got one of those later) and said, this is where the work is. You might be lucky enough to be asked to a series of parties but if you're going to too many of those, you're not where you're needed, at the work table, at the typewriter, as it were.

Fiction writers in order to meet their discipline write a minimum of words per day. I suppose some of the poets do as well. I don't. There are moments when I don't want to get near the writing process. I hope to hell something is distilling in me at those times for future hootenanny guest spots.

It's a nebulous crap-shoot, this process. Bukowski might not be spoken of by them who supposedly know in the same cadences as maybe Dante, or Chaucer. They were poet poets.

But Dante liberated his readers because instead of shooting his metaphors at them in Latin, which was the current craze, he did it in Tuscan, his local ground dialect which became Italian as we know it.

Chaucer, likewise, dealt his public a garrulous enough deck of Middle English, as opposed to French, which the upwardly mobile poets of his time sung and marched to. He gave his public, well, those of them who might not have known French well enough to play the poet/reader game, something to cheer about.

Bukowski, as Woody Guthrie did, wrote about everything in his day by day twirl. Not all of your subjects can be the Subject of Poetry for All Time to Come. Don't hold back. Write about anything and everything and the good dance will wobble through.

He'd simply juggle the laughing/crying yin yang clown prince dance floor. Years ago in San Francisco, when I was cutting my Masters molar, I saw him do a read downtown. There was a cactus on stage. Some obstreperous wag kept haranguing Bukowski. At one point he asked, "Bukowski, what does the cactus represent?" Bukowski said, "Give me a few moments to think about it." Later on some other waif called out, "What's Jesus Christ?" "The cactus," said Bukowski, "he'll stick you every time." He flicked an ash onto the cactus.

Some overwrought, educated fool wrote a review of that reading. The fool fell into the doomed drinking poet myth. Claimed the Bukowski I saw on stage was a doomed poet. Shucks. I knew better and different. Jesus might stick you every time, but you learn from such sticking that your foot nerves are alive and in the game.

A few days ago I saw a vintage TV show featuring the Rat Pack from 1965. You know those guys. Sinatra, Martin, Davis Jr. They ran an unnecessary disclaimer on it, saying how some of the stuff said and mentioned may not be appreciated in this holy year of hey now 1997 (we've come a long way I guess) but it was a signature of the times, blah absurdity. The main thing was the Rat Pack, politically correct or not (whatever that is—Christ, these folks were entertainers, if I remember, and not politicians) were Having Fun. Between themselves and with the audience.

Bukowski was having fun at that reading. No doomed poet there. All in the mind of that over-educated cerebral twit who wanted to see a doomed poet when he or she penned that review.

Bukowski could laugh with himself, not at himself. Poetry, to survive, as any art, needs to be able to step outside of its holier than whatever cathedral, and lower its pants and now and then say, "Told you so, yuck, yuck, yuck."

The war you see is ongoing. In order to fight it, you have to be much larger than politically correct. Was Bukowski an empathetic daddy who felt? Try Last Days of the Suicide Kid or Death of an Idiot.

As S.A. Griffin, the Zen caddy master says, "You write for

yourself, not the unknown demographic audience." They won't be taking our poems to some sneak reading in Encino and then have the customers fill out lobby cards. "Could you change those last six lines, please?"

Pick up the world, roll it around in the history of your hands. It feels good. It burns. It laughs. It bleeds. Tell me about it. How the weather calls on your skin. What words it uses. Bukowski painted pictures and he lived in Los Angeles. My hotel.

He sang sweet love songs, my friend. He played the blues and knocked cans over at night to the tune of I am a Writer living in the deep blue language.

I sit here, about to back out of this piece. I will do it quietly. There is a music in the bedrock. It keeps us afloat. Bukowski played his sax. A wind began to grin. Darling, don't hate me too much, because I love you so long I'll still be singing your name when the handcuffs come down from Mount Olympus.

Keep singing.

(***Ed. note:*** *There's not much that I can say about Scott, except that he's a fine poet and one-helluva beef-cake, so any of you ladies who are interested, take note.*)

No Mistakes – *February 1998*

WORDS HOP UP FROM NERVE ENDS. Words claim they can cook you the most holy of omelets for this ongoing breakfast of the head and the planet below. Good morning. My name is nobody in particular and I live in my bloodstream. The ongoing argument of humanity versus all non-human is a moot one. As George Carlin wryly observes, the planet has outlived dinosaurs, and will outlive us. Arrogant, we presume that if we disappear, the earth will as well. Words raise their fleeting hands at the back of the classroom, demand they be rendered in some audible floor show of tongue and dream. Words such as metaphor, lyric, hallelujah, music. I hope you mean it baby. Words such as kill, hate, fuck. This issue features S. A. Griffin on sax, doing a duet with Raindog. S. A. has hanging in his theater of the soul (apartment) "Fuck Hate." Which is the bad word? Bukowski and Richmond, Steve. Fighting dance hall queens and riverboat gamblers of luck and love. Hate, of course, is a bad word, but the people who take away your license to sing decree that fuck is evil. Just a word, honey. An overdone one at that. Joe Pesci and Robert De Niro in a Scorsese parade. The most holy of omelets, broken from the egg mosaic.

Words call you collect when you cannot pay your phone bill. What can you do? But let the rain fall on your soul and remember that we are not dead until we call ourselves dead. The planet will be here in fifty years in some form. Maybe not us, but it will. I am not arrogant enough to claim any words I create in my kitchen will matter in the long run, but the race I'm clocking is the here-to-now bebop, and sometimes my words will make the coffee percolate a little less bitter.

You will hear S. A. and Raindog sing to each other in this issue of Lummox. Raindog takes off his top hat and out come rabbits of I want you to name your tune honey, and then wail it out in these pages. S, A. has been writing music for years and years, and you can hear him taking the 7 dwarfs out for a good time, I have been with those dwarfs, and when Snow White went missing in action, we got on our skateboards of time and space and went flying in all directions trying to get the chandelier back on the ceiling before midnight. Words snap their memory and the circus becomes a way of hearing. Climb up the faltering steps, climb up the precarious road, and be prepared to check yourself out in the glorious republic of I am alive. I am sentient, I am clown, I am jurist, I am music, I am skin, I am just whoever the fuck it is I am, and no more, no less.

Raindog said write something about creativity. Creativity is its own city. Robert Viharo is true when he says there is No Method (as in Method Acting), that what works for one, may not work for the other, but whatever it is, it is unique and central to each person. Creativity has no phone book and dictionary, has no parole officer, or interpreter. It is its own planet, decade, house, mind.

Each of us, simply sort of half-assed put, is our own book. Each of us, our own subject matter. Everything is risk. Everything is exploration. Everything is not knowing. Everything is gamble. Everything is nothing but the moment. The moment has no pedigree, background, future. It is what we are in the actual what we are.

There are no mistakes. It is all recovery.

There are no mistakes. It is all song.

transfusion of a soul – *April 1998 (All Poetry Issue)*

to release
one's
self
is like
the cutting of
scars
which have
grown
over 10 years skin.

leathery tough
to
thin blade of
mind doctor
incision
ready to make.
prodding at
past child
lost within
pierces arteries
bleeding
ventricles of
madness.

an existence hearts and minds
their pasts, together they attempt to
walk through futures that may
or may not be kind to them some men and women pass
one another finally in the long ongoing hallway
they pass their best intentions
as a duet this does not make them any
less valuable for the soloist's soul is a long
term breath unit
tonight in the large arteries of this city

men and women pass each other in silence
and their hearts are maddened and made
human by longing
men and women share names and have
children
and instruments are making noise in their tissue
tonight finally love gets up from a tiny
table and lights a cigarette
it is lonely perhaps or perhaps full of
smiling
perhaps it is crooked or wide and even
in the perplexed study of all lighting
we are thin shadows of ongoing color
hear the blood going slow and soft
through the tension of the hours
and yet we all keep dreaming forward
into the late night early morning
long ongoing seconds of
hello

Just What A National Poetry Month *Might* Mean – *June 1998*

GOOD DAY. MY FELLOW WORDSMITHS. I hope you are dancing well out there in the large unwieldy world. It's National Poetry month (well, I'm writing this in April. Obviously by the time it appears in print this will have all gone off.) and I have come to wonder about such an entity.

April usually means tax time. Eliot, who was a poet, or claimed he was such, called April the cruelest month. I guess he had trouble with the IRS, or the English version of such. Just joking. Poets can do that, joke. I'm just wondering how come April got picked. Why not June with the beginning strumming chords of summer wine?

I know we have a poet laureate here. The poet laureate position is something we borrowed from England. I suppose we figured somewhere on the national level of looking and hearing that if it worked okay for England we should do it too. The lucky lady or guy who gets that position should feel honored, obviously, it being the highest chair a poet could choose to try and sit on in the whole landscape of chairs and such.

A poet laureate, in honoring their position, has to do at least one lecture about the art of poetry. I had a weird image of me, being a laureate, doing some kind of rap to the combined House and Senate about the process, whatever the hell the process is. I mean, since it is a process, you really can't stop it long enough to trap its essence in something as wondrously mundane as words.

Let's face it. The moment is always going to be so much faster. By the time we try to freeze it and then write about it, it's gone, baby. Adios.

We can, however, work from our feelings and thoughts. That's the canvas we so-called artists are painting in. No matter how obstreperous, weird, angular, brittle, goofy and redundant we might be in our collective war or attempted peace with the universe, we all have feelings and thoughts.

Fine enough. I mean. I'd be all finished with my sought for one lecture a year so fast we could all go out onto the steps of the Capitol and get into some scat work.

The subject of your poetry is how you feel and think. Hear, dream, dance.

The federal government really must like poetry. To actually pull one of the twelve months to the side and sit it down, wave a finger in its face, and say you are National Poetry Month, is something marvelous, maybe.

Feelings, thoughts. We all share them. This is a given. So a few of us selected weird ones figure we can share our thoughts and feelings in words. Rather than music notes, paint, clay, dance.

We then fall into the writing ark. Fiction people on the upper berth, as they are apt to get a hopeful publishing deal maybe, or a movie deal. I haven't seen too many films based on poems. There have been a few. Joseph Moncure March's poem The Set Up became the basis of a pretty damn good Robert Wise film with Robert Ryan and Audrey Totter.

But let's give the fiction people the upper berth and window view of the ocean as the writing ark sets out on its exploration. The novelists get the real top. The short story people, the middle. The poets, well, the bottom bunk is okay with me. Don't have to crawl down too far when I got to get up during the night to use the bathroom.

Do they have a National Short Story Month?

They are very difficult to write, short stories. For me, anyhow.

Do you look at a poet differently than usual during National Poetry Month? So far my customers at work look at me as if nothing unusual was afoot.

The days just stumble along as eclectically goofy as they are apt.

Does a poet laureate read more intensely than a non-poet laureate?

These are all random thoughts and feelings, mind you. I know you got random feelings and thoughts. Instead of doing something constructive like writing a poem or reading some fine book, I am putting my thoughts and feelings down in this essay. I don't write essays very often. My attempts at thoughts and feelings are more scattered and unfocused than a practical essay would have brought to the table.

Maybe I should just write a poem instead.

National Poetry Month called up and said your phone is stupid and I said sure it is, because a stupid phone is a democratic phone. National Poetry Month asked my sister out for a date. She looked at the sky and tossed her switchblade way up into it.

No. Forget writing a poem. I don't feel the poem coming on right now. Except to a poet, everything is a poem. So that's a big lie.

The late great Texas songwriter Townes Van Zandt (a poet) is in the CD machine talking at me as I write this article. If he were alive today I would ask the government to make him a poet laureate. Or a songwriter laureate. Or a laureate laureate.

Laureate and Hearty were a fine comedy team.

There is a light in your dark volleyball court. The light has a friend under each arm. They all know the mangled words to some hip folk song that makes your skin grow trees. Sing it now with me if you can, and I know you can, because you are all thoughts and feelings, as the great Robert Viharo dancing man says.

I know you know the words. Hum along with your blood now as we sing this one together.

Won't you grab the windmill, my honey, and let the gravity become a verb of Jazz in the maybe I will get through this pain maybe I won't demolition derby hope.

The poets are rivers of noisy silt. The poets are basketball playoffs that never are won or lost. The moment is a circus in which all the clowns are scientists of love.

It's National Poetry Month. Give yourself a kiss and we'll run into each other soon enough on the dance floor. Until then keep radiating.

Russian Dissident Hootenanny – *August 1998*

I DON'T REMEMBER HOW I GOT IT, BACK IN the seventies when I was earning my MA piece of paper at San Francisco State University, I became the owner of a Charles Bukowski T-shirt.

It didn't have any major fancy label attached to it, but it sure did have a wondrous large reproduction of Buk's face in close up all over the front.

I tend to favor T-shirts (good thing I don't live in a cold climate) and I wore that thing so much, finally it died of old age.

It's a pity T-shirts get holes in them.

Once, while wearing shirt Bukowski, somebody asked me if he was a Russian Dissident. I said No, he's actually a poet in Los Angeles, but then, maybe if you believe in alternative ongoing realities, he might have been a Russian dissident along-side his Los Angeles poet fiction writer persona.

My buddy and ex-prof Dan Langton at State said, "You know how they make those shirts? They get him shitfaced and then he passes out face first on the press and they run off a hundred or so, then they get him shitfaced all over again and...etc. etc. etc"

When my first collection of poems came out thanks to Dave Smith and Ouija Madness Press, "Mr. Mumps," I got my cover photo taken at the now defunct Danny's Oki Dog joint on Santa Monica near Gardner, wearing this shirt. Bill Wilner took the photo and afterwards we stumbled off to the Tiffany theater on Sunset to see a Polish movie fraught with metaphor and political fervor.

It was one of those Man of movies, you know, Man of Iron, Man of Stone.

Some time hence, while toiling at my job at Brentwood Bookshop (now Dutton's) my last and only customer was none other than Bob

Dylan, another L.A. poet, and perhaps ongoing Russian Dissident. Not wanting to get in his face, and knowing his reputation for wariness, I let Dylan have the run of the store (at that time just one room) and he saw my book on the counter (one of the benefits of working the bookstore trade) and the first words from his soul were:

"Where did you get the Bukowski shirt?"

I've written enough poems in honor of Bukowski's long range race for the roses that didn't exist, yet smell so damnably captivating. Every year Raindog puts out the Bukowski issue of LUMMOX and it's hard not repeating your traces. I could tell you that Bukowski made it okay for me to write in a speech even I could understand. I've done that already. I wish I still had that shirt. I got others with his artistic facsimile on them, but I like to think this particular shirt, the one that Langton made fun of, actually held its own for years and years in an era of Planet Hollywood and Hard Rock Cafe things. Christ, could you actually wear a shirt sponsoring a place that is so noisy you couldn't even hear yourself fart after eating a mediocre hamburger?

Poetry is a hard business. At the same time it can be so crazily easy. You have to let go, you have to clear your head of the sludge and ego debris and let yourself embrace the ongoing whatever.

Wales has Dylan Thomas. Ireland has Yeats and so many others. England has Auden and a Yankee who checked out named Eliot. The U. S. at large has Whitman, Williams, Stevens (his U. S. is of the mind) and I guess Frost and Ginsberg, to a degree, but lowly, geeky Los Angeles, the joint nobody wants to own up to as having any generic potential?

Stuart Perkoff we got, and Charles Bukowski. I doubt when these folks checked out, they got the coverage that Princess Diana has. Or even Sonny Bono. Nothing against those folks, mind you. I never had a Stuart Perkoff shirt, but if you showed me one, I just might buy it.

Reviews – *December 1998*

Tomorrow
Starring Robert Duvall/Olga Bellin.
Stark yet lyrical rendering of William Faulkner short story. Sparse, yet illuminating and haunting.

Wanda
A film by Barbara Loden. Natural investigation of a woman searching for sustenance. Written and Directed and Staring Loden (she was married to Elia Kazan)this is an altogether encompassing honest voyage.

Angelo My Love
Robert Duvall directed this energetic exploration of real gypsies living in New York. Duvall apparently saw Angelo on the street and was captivated. He took a year and wrote a script and the gypsies actually came to work. The camera never gets in the way of the vital energy. A dance throughout.

Sweet Smell of Success
Britisher Alexander Mackendrick turns his eye on New York and gives us a destructive powerful relationship between a powerful gossip columnist (Burt Lancaster) and a sleazy press agent (Tony Curtis). Tony Curtis' best work. Lancaster's character is a fictional Walter Winchell. The script by Clifford Odets and Ernest Lehman/taken from Lehman's novella, zips, zings, zaps, and takes you upside down. A character in Barry Levinson's Diner ran around quoting this film at length.

Ace in the Hole aka The Big Carnival
Billy Wilder's bleak investigation of what happens when the media gets out of hand by making the event, and not simply reporting it. This came out in the early fifties and nobody wanted to pay to examine its hard edged truth. Very timely and ahead of its time. Kirk Douglas, Jan Sterling, Porter Hall, Robert Arthur, Richard Benedict, and Ray Teal.

Tunes of Glory
Alec Guinness and John Mills excel in this postwar drama of two officers at odds in which way their military command should go. What does a war time army do to occupy itself when there is no war? Directed by Ronald Neame, from James Kenaway's novel. Haunting throughout. Susannah York's first film.

Odd Man Out
James Mason as a dying IRA man struggling to stay alive in the streets of Dublin. Directed by Sir Carol Reed. One of the best of all time.

Blood Meridian by Cormac McCarthy
Poetic yet violent account of life in the 19th Century American southwest. Musically brutal and unflinching.

The Assault by Harry Mulisch
A novel about a horrible act of World War Two and its ongoing ramifications as the years go by…The basis of a later film.

Men with Guns
John Sayles' latest film. Quiet, yet forceful. Shot in Spanish and Indian dialect. Can one actually know one's country? An odyssey of awakening for its main character, a cerebral big city doctor, who realizes he can't even understand the Indians of his own country's villages. Lyrical, and resonating.

The Tall T
Budd Boetticher's version of an Elmore Leonard short story(The Captives).Laconic Randolph Scott, villainous Richard Boone(but with an ache to shoot higher than just being a villain), Maureen O'Sullivan,and Henry Silva as a cold blooded killer who can't even remember if he ever shot a woman or not. One of the best Scott-Boetticher-Burt Kennedy collaborations.

Ride the High Country
Before Peckinpah did the Wild Bunch to slam the door closed on the sixties, there was this gem of 1962, exploring themes that Peckinpah

would later elaborate upon in the Bunch. Joel McCrea and Randolph Scott, two B western icons, appear for the first and last time together as aging lawmen attempting to finish one last job. Time has taken its toll on the way Scott views the world, and that toll leads to conflict that will forever change his relationship with McCrea. Mariette Hartley's first film and look for Warren Oates as one of the nefarious Hammond brothers. Long a Peckinpah regular, Oates was one of the best character actors around.

What Work Is by Philip Levine
Levine is an accessible poet who has never forgot his working class history (he used to work the blue collar auto line in Detroit).His poems are always filled with humans, and they are never buried by overuse of language. The title poem in this collection might make you cry a bit.

Number two live Dinner
Robert Earl Keen
Keen, a contemporary of Lyle Lovett, shines in this live album of songs. Merry Christmas from the Family, Mariano, and a humorous intro to the Road Goes on Forever and then the song itself with a blistering Bryan Duckworth fiddle sequence.

Diamonds in the Rough and John Prine
John Prine
Actually any Prine. But these are the first two collections and will be a fine beginning to those who want to explore. The first album alone, JP is filled with songs that have become classics ... Donald and Lydia, Angel from Montgomery, Sam Stone, Illegal Smile...

The Rose of the San Joaquin
Tom Russell
Some strong Russell here. His cover of Chris Gaffney's In The Garden; Out in California (co written with Dave Alvin), and a fine version of Tramps and Hawkers (traditional tune, words by Jim Ringer).

Scott Wannberg Interview - *January 1999*

*(**Editor's note:** Scott, a former memory in the Carma Bums—a traveling road show of poetry and performance, which toured the western US from 1989 to 2009—is a fixture in not only the L.A. poetry scene, but Dutton's of Brentwood, as well. He has read at countless venues around L.A., was one of the original "rock poets" and is a long time and much revered friend of many of L.A.'s best poets and this editor. One of those poets, S.A. Griffin is often referred to in this interview as "SA." He and Scott go back many years.)*

RD: *What is your history?*

SW: I was born a Scandinavian white man in Santa Monica... not affluent but I never went hungry, I mean the old man worked as an Aerospace engineer, so that was good money. My mother was a nurse, so they both worked, it was a workin' family. Again it was a middle class family, we lived in suburbia, until my parents broke up (I was in Elementary School). Nothing ornate. I lived in houses until they broke up, then I lived in apartments.

RD: *Did you grow up In Santa Monica?*

SW: No. I was born there but grew up in the Valley, (ha ha) the nebulous San Fernando Valley, which was a lot less crowded than it is now; in Granada Hills, Northridge, Panorama City. I don't know why 'cause the old man worked over here, but maybe he liked the commute... I dunno. I pretty much lived with my mom after they broke up, until her third husband and then I moved over here with the old man and (ha ha) I'm still living with him now... no one wants to take him off my hands (ha ha). You know it's the old story.

RD: *Didn't you go to San Francisco State?*

Scott was named "LUMMOX of the Year" in 1999.

SW: Yeah, I went there 'cause it was one of the few schools that I knew that was offering a degree in Creative Writing. It sounded like something I could make work. And I'd never been north, I'd heard a lot about it, I wanted to explore northern California, so I went up to SF State to get my BA and MA.

RD: *So when were you up there?*

SW: Uh, I went up there in 72, got the BA in 74, took some time off (the MA program was very small and I missed the first go-round), and got my MA in 76, I believe.

RD: *Was that helpful?*

SW: (ha ha) Not necessarily... I know that I could have pursued a teaching position at one of the junior colleges, but I had no empathy for it.

RD: *So you came back to L.A. and did...what?*

SW: Well, I worked in a drive in and as an usher in a theater (I could tell you some stories!) and I worked in an independent bookstore, and I just didn't see the need to teach. I like books. So far, I'm doing okay here [at Dutton's].

RD: *How long have you been at Dutton's?*

SW: I've been here since the beginning. And before it was Dutton's, I worked for Lou Virgil starting in 1980 – Doug [Dutton] took it over in '84. I had a chance to work with this guy upstairs doing import-export for better pay, but I was totally lost. This guy'd been doing it for years and I just had no empathy for it. So I came back down because I wanted to work with the books. So here I am.

RD: *So, Dutton's is your life?*

SW: When I leave this place, I do not take it home with me!

RD: *Okay. When you write, does the workplace creep into your writing?*

SW: What do you mean?

RD: *Well, Fred Voss, for example, has made quite a reputation writing about being a machinist at "GoodStone". And other people use the workplace as a focal point for their writing... do you?*

SW: Well, I do on occasion write about working retail, but it's very seldom. This job doesn't intrude on my life, it's not like I'm going to get a call in the middle of the night saying, "We're going to need something for tomorrow's meeting." 'Cause I got no meeting tomorrow! Maybe I'd have more money, but I'm doing okay.

RD: *It's not the road that everybody takes, then.*

SW: No. But I can still do my one or two seconds worth of teaching here, if some youth comes in looking for suggestions for a book, I can make a point or two. We do get asked, on occasion, what we like (to read) here.

RD: *So, when did you hook up with SA Griffin?*

SW: It was about a year after I started at Dutton's. I went to a reading at The Masters Club and I met Jim Burns (who edited the Shatter Sheet—a kind of poetry calendar of the time) and SA Griffin was helping him to put it out. I didn't know anything about him or the Lost Tribe or Doug (Knott) and Mike (Molett) and Mike (Bruner). I came back a few more times, met some people there and one thing led to another, eventually I met SA at a club called X=Art.

SA had seen me at the Anti-Club doing my piece called the "Ed Meese Blues" and he liked it. I started doing stuff with SA and Mike Bruner all over, like we did a little improvisation with sheet music (where if the song was a torch song they'd do a poem like that) one night at At My Place in Santa Monica. I liked doing that kind of thing. This led to our hitting it off and that's where it began.

RD: *So, had you already been writing?*

SW: Oh yeah, since college. But it wasn't me, I wasn't good at writing the form stuff, I had no empathy for rhyme or that other stuff... not that there's anything wrong with it. If you can write a sestina, then you should do that. Me, I liked the free form. All poetry boils down to this: you can say whatever you can say, the best way you say it, in the form you say it in.

RD: *Had you been doing poetry readings at that point?*

SW: Yeah. Here and there. I did readings at places like Deja Vu (where the owner didn't like poets and would walk out whenever they read) and other places, all gone now. In fact, by that time, I had also been in Shatter Sheet, as well. I was in an ongoing anthology called Tsunami and did various publication readings around town.

RD: *Was it pretty thin, reading-wise?*

SW: No, it was just different. Venues come and go and the cycle changes. At that time SA was doing readings at a place called The Water. And there was always Beyond Baroque (in Venice), I read at Gorky's. All over. It comes and goes. But this coffeehouse thing is popular now, though I'm not a big fan of readings in coffeehouses because you have all that noise interfering with your reading. I much prefer book stores or libraries where people are there to listen. I remember Steve Goldman had a reading down in Venice, off the boardwalk and I read there along with Dennis Holt and Garret Hawkins and then he moved it over to the old Venice jail (next to where Beyond Baroque is) and I read there.

RD: *So, you read at Beyond Baroque at its original location?*

SW: Yes, when it was on West Washington. It was much more empathetic, like going into George's (George Drury Smith, founder and owner of the building that first housed Beyond Baroque) old, dusty library. The readings were in the book room, surrounded by books. I liked it then. A lot of people went through that Venice Poetry Workshop that met on Wednesdays, Tom Waits, Exene, John Doe, not to mention a few poets, too.

RD: When you met SA, there was a connection between you. What was that about?

SW: Yeah, I was always willing to get off paper and explore the process. I liked the blend of printed material and/or memorized material (though I hate to memorize) and the unknown... to be truly spontaneous in the moment. Yeah, I've always been open to that. I don't fear it, 'cause you can't fear something you don't judge. There's nothing wrong with having a really firm floor to stand on, before you lift a leg, you need that, but then again there's also nothing wrong with falling down! It's not for everyone. I've always believed if something don't work, do something else!

RD: How did the Carma Bums come about?

SW: SA went to Colorado to shoot a movie and he met some people up there doing this spontaneous improvisation stuff and when he came back to LA, he got together with me and some of the other members of the Lost Tribe. They had been doing these workshops with Scott Kellman, using these techniques designed to help performers (not so much actors). We began to employ these techniques in our own work, though I was less familiar with these techniques. Sometimes it didn't work out as planned.

RD: When you are in the moment, what's that like?

SW: There's a tendency to want to rush to the goal, but there is no need to. The goal is right there with you. But this is not an easy concept to get. The audience is part of the show, not some separate part. Make them part of the event. The event begins before the show starts. The event is the show. When we went on the road, the shows were really just an excuse to go on the road!

RD: *I can only compare what you're saying to the shows that I do with The CasioTones. Invariably Marshall (Astor) will ask me, "how's the show going?" And I won't be able to tell him, I won't know until I hear a tape of the show, 'cause I'm in the moment, usually lost there on purpose.*

SW: Yes, it's about listening. It's why SA and I are Deadheads. It's all about being fluid. You have to be aware that it's not just you, but then again you have to also be aware that it can be anything and it can also be you and it can go anywhere, at anytime.

RD: *So creativity is a fluid experience?*

SW: Yes. There were moments with the Carma Bums where I felt we were hamstrung by retreating into those things (Kellman's "centering" exercises). I would rather have let the thing dangle. If the show had reached a moment where it was dead air or dead space or nobody was doing a piece, that was okay, and yet, we felt that we had better do something, like one of those Scott Kellman exercises. Sometimes, there's nothing wrong with the dead moment, just let it dangle. It can't be the same thing everytime. And if you want professional, slick, no-risk, guaranteed safety for each performance then you're doing yourself and your audience an injustice; because as much as you'd like to have a professional, slick show, it can't be the same thing everytime. You have to dance with it, you have to commit yourself to go with it, wherever it takes you.

RD: *Have you been typecast as a Carma Bum? And is that an obstacle?*

SW: I think I have been. If SA and I do some reading now, people wonder if it might be a "Bum" thing, and I have to say, "no, it's just me and SA." It's a lazy way to identify you, by someone who doesn't really know your work. It's like saying that Bukowski was an L.A. writer, so every writer from L.A. wants to be like him. I wouldn't say that Harry Northup wants to be like him, and he's an L.A. writer. I'm certainly not like him and I'm an L.A. writer. Nor, for that matter is SA like him, or you, and yet, we all are big fans of his writing... it's such a cliché to say someone is a Bukowski-wannabe, or a Frank O'Hara wannabe, or a Delmore Schwartz wannabe, I don't know. It doesn't tell me anything about the writer or the material.

RD: There's the Beat school and the Meat school and...

SW: But none of that tells me anything. Kerouac and Ginsberg wrote very differently. And Burroughs, it's like reading wacky, stream-of-consciousness, Joyce-like, non-linear, three dimensional wow...

RD: You seem to be able to free-associate without end. Is this something that you've always done?

SW: It may have been dormant when I was a kid, everybody was pretty much here-and-now... but when I got older and found like-minded people, 'cause you really need to be with people who are similar to find out if it will work. I started tapping into that in the '70s, in college and after. I used to hang out with Steve Goldman and he can do it, SA does it, Doug Knott does it to a degree.

RD: Is it like shtick?

SW: Naw. Shtick is having it mapped out, knowing the danger points, the ever-reliable, the accustomed-to. Shtick is what works. If you're in the moment, you don't know what works and you don't know where the danger points are, because you're just going there blankly — you may hit a wall or you may hold your nose and go the other way. There are people who are really good at it, like Cathy Brewer, she can blow! I've heard her do the "rap" at shows.

RD: What's that.

SW: Free association and the rap, to me, are the same thing. It's spontaneous language, spontaneous use of words, a narrative of sorts.

RD: Is there a difference between the way you write a poem or prose piece and the way that you do a rap? I mean, beyond the fact that you write down a poem and you "speak" the rap. Is there a difference beyond that?

SW: If I'm writing a piece, a poem, the energy's definitely got to be there (the energy's not that changeable) and, while free association can go anywhere, if I'm trying to write a poem about something, I suppose there's going to be a theme, a reason to sit down and write in the first place.

RD: *Like the poem Scarecrow.*

SW: Yes. A poem is more of an attempt to take the energy and shape it in such a way, that it becomes something. That's not to say that the verbal rap is not becoming something. But the attempt is more cognizant in the poem to try and shape it into some kind of accessible "end" piece; to take the theme, mood, color, and move it somewhere and, then when you're there, to get out of it. Whereas the rap could be on-going, or absurd, or totally non-linear.

RD: Do you have a preference between writing and rapping?

SW: I think they are both equally demanding and both equally rewarding. I like them both, but I think I can get away with more on the written thing. The verbal always peters out, it's more difficult than on paper. It is, after all, about imagery. And imagery is not easy and yet we live in nothing but.

RD: *So true.*

SW: Jack Grapes once said that in writing, it's important to keep yourself open, to keep yourself available to seeing the world differently. You don't need to know what you are going to write, just write what you see and edit it later. I agree with this.

* * *

(As LUMMOX of the Year, Scott will receive a free year of LUMMOX Journal, *a chapbook of his poetry + 30 copies, a special edition T-Shirt and a NEW CAR— kidding!)*

Littleton - *1999*

the blood runs out of speech
the hole in I Meant Better widens
come now, can you accomplish the soft
shoe?
17 faces on page one of the local paper this morning
they won t be making the jubilee their millennium has come and
gone Eric Harris and Dylan Klebold handed them a different
manuscript the cursor snaps in half from trying to
deal with too much input the lines are down
even the ones that were never really up the motels of the heart are
burning up terror is really not an aphrodisiac Columbine High
becomes Kosovo the machinery falls apart the better mousetrap
has been built so
well it
prevails all night long
when this poet went to high school it
fist fights and
maybe just maybe a knife fight
technology has arrived surely
Harris and Klebold did their weaponry proud
the lines snap at your heels in the electric forgive me
handed them a manuscript that meant to go down different
12 young good time faces and one teacher
handed them a no exit scenario
nobody wanted to claim the directing chore
the motels of my eyes are burning
nobody need bother to check in
the lines cannot hold
the lines cannot sing
let me follow your line
let me follow your fear
the hails of learning are learned into the bones
learned burning and deep
is it safe?

Is it safe?
Fuck no, it is never safe and never will be safe
the howling unmerciful glee club is out on the prowl
full body armor intact
they cut you down for being alive
they cut you down and say it's because you don't understand
Harris and Klebold, if they really wanted love
well, I would have gotten them drunk and then
stoned but they Would have probably cut me down
because everything to them Was just cuttable
nothing prevails
but the never ending search for something that
prevails
in the hot ice bucket
in the collapsing vernacular
you will find the dance hall in search of your love
in the bewildered chest haranguing
in the speeches to come
even the president gets into it
come quick solve the problem
get the guns out of our schools
get the guns out of our homes
get the guns out of our lovemaking
in the dark alley of I want to know you
in the dark valley of I want to kill you
there must be a chance to
hear
there must be a Way to see
Harris and Klebold and .Milosevic
all got derailed on their way to the soiree
they lost the chance to hear and see
in the bottomless credit card
in the wistful horror
the ushers and usherettes glow in the painful

radioactive dark
they are thin and dapper
get the fucking guns out of our love
get the knife out of our hope
get the ax out of your jazz music
in the empty dark hours of hope
in the community of Littleton, Colorado
where ethnic cleansing became a tone poem
come on baby let s play awhile
come on baby take off your pain
come on baby there s room for you and me
in the lockup of love
in the frozen hours of I don't want to become a face on page
one of the L.A. Times
I don't want to become a statistic for the president to
bewail
come on baby reach out across the pit of fire
come on baby reach out and let me find you in the
last hours of our world
the millennium is moaning bloody at the door
it is Well armed and doesn't like a lot of folks
you best duck and cover
the bomb is falling
the bomb is always falling
I love you anyway
I love you despite myself
the bomb is falling all the time
you just got to know how to see it
hear it
and know how to run

poetry says yes - *September/October 2005*

no denying it
standing there on the tip of the tongue
enough rabble rousing
time to imbibe in metaphor
poetry says you bet
the weather might even be kind
who's to say?
The earth claims it's not flat
let it sing then and we can be the judge
the earth begins to chortle
poetry says of course
no strain indeed
the muscles seem to work
name the day and night
name the way you part your hair
as the mountains align themselves
to your favorite tune.

10/07/05

Where the rivers run - *March/April 2006*

Sooner or later the music in your wounded heart
will work its way through the bones of ongoing hope
where the rivers run and the heart finds you in time
to prevent freezing.
The front door of my eyes open wide
and seeing can be believing.
The painted sky is a bit chipped
but latitude and longitude can still
tell time. Sooner or later the
dance in your wounded head will
find its rhythm where those rivers run
and all is vulnerable with love.

Sheree Rose

The Revolution Has Been Remaindered - *March/April 2005*

sight seers needed,
apply on your head,
murder carves its heart in the giving tree
hold onto your one last match
the dark is strutting around fierce

not enough morphine to go around
raise your vulnerable head to the heat
magic once called you its friend
embrace it if you can, find it in your soul,
the revolution has been remaindered…

in the back room of the drunk city
where the tall men shrink
i greet you in a language
that will make your ear giggle

Mahatma Gandhi on skateboards
Will teach you grace
as the artillery opens up its
heart

in the long ago sometime soon end of things
in the dumpsters of the forgotten
in the shadow and fog of your lucidity
in the double-talk downsize
in the eyeless don't make wondrous guide dogs
will the promises keep their skin on ,
will the love's biopsy come back negative

come over to the wet bar
come over and be tested
we'll down all the liquor that made the Earth movable
we'll toast the new armada

when the dead and the dying get their own network
when the Constitution rolls itself up in a joint and inhales
when the last wagon decides never to leave
in the resonant can't hear you rhythm
in the long walk to the end of dreaming
will the clowns make you genuinely laugh

i put the earth in my right pocket
i put the earth on hold
i put the earth in my underwear
i put the earth in a strait-jacket
the earth is my best friend
the earth cooks for me
and the dishes?
Do they ever get done?

They'll be over soon to do you right
they'll put the fear of God into your dog's tail
my dog doesn't believe in their God
it's gonna be a long night.

The Dove Has Fangs - *September/October 2004*

They sent me a dove, or so they claimed.
Please let us know if you love our dove.
Their dove has fangs.
It bit its way out of its cage,
and was big time belligerent.
I sent that dove packing,
Wrote Bush and Cheney an angry letter.
How come you sent me a dove with fangs, boys?
Fangs are good to protect you from terror,
they answered. We want to protect you from
the terror that lives in your blood every second.
You guys must be way too stoned.
Doves don't have fangs.
And Terror? Everywhere you go you might find it.
Or have it find you. But Doves, repeat,
do not have fangs. I got crooked teeth, myself.
The next time they claim something is what it isn't,
I just might have to bite down.

the possibility of life – *October 2003*

the civil war is over
the uncivil war is almost over as well
life is sick and tired of all this killing
life got angry and shoved killing against a wall
slapped it around
said get it together asshole

all this week it's been stay alive week on cable
people who claim they are still alive
are everywhere you turn
sometimes i have my doubts
doubts are okay
they just mean you are still human

are you still human?
Did you explore your experience
did you find yourself alive and taking in air
life is still possible
life tossed death head first through an upper floor window
life was that pissed off
death fell a long way down
and landed on all the candidates for governor in California
squishing them all to oblivious bits

it made the recall unnecessary
and life yawned, popped in a DVD of
Humphrey Bogart in Treasure of the Sierra Madre
go get em John Huston yippie

i sort of woke up then
and became another noun running around
searching for a verb to say hello to

the Earth got pulled over for
impersonating a profound planet
it reached for its license
life is still possible, it sang
and we all agree
that yes
sometimes
when you least expect it
it surely is

8/17/03

send out for a crying room that can hold water – *April 2003*

razor blades they hide in the free food
best go get a protection shield for your mouth
get a crying room that will hold water

sent the last good boy out for coffee
and a bagel some days ago
guess he didn't make it

i look out the window, down below
to the ever widening hole in the intersection

does anyone live at the bottom of that hole
does anyone live

guess we'll have to go out and get our own coffee and bagel

i thought about coming here to love you
but they handed me a lot of papers at the door
filled with instructions that would get
us to where we thought we had to go

nowhere in those instructions
did i see anything about it being legal
for me to come here to love you

guess i'm going to have to break the law

otherwise i'd have to hate you

am not ready to do that
give me time maybe

no

don't give me any time

give me your hand, though
don't know where our hands will take the rest of us
but let's start there

sort of simple, really

without thinking
just stick out your arm

Without thinking
explore your heart

3/23/03

John Prine Rap – *June 2002*

SARDONIC BARE FEET MARKING ENRICHING meter on the possibility at work in Earth. John Prine, former Chicago mailman, now Oh Boy Records incarnate singing, seeing, dreaming, strumming, acting, being... yes, indeed.

In 1971 his debut album, John Prine. Crawled luxuriously into your empathetic hope of a bloodstream and began to build cities of the heart within your own heart, and here it is 2002 and the poetry and skin are intact with an affinity for life and all the harsh rooms of love that try to hold their own there.

Playful river, hard rock, painful wound, sustaining love, torn skin of attempted breathing, one deep canyon of a Zen moment, Prine is all of this, and more, the sum of all the parts of an artist, an artist who allows you to blend in with all the variable elements of the world.

Steve Goodman lives on in his bare feet.

The hard streets of the world trying to learn itself, they are made that much easier to handle through such engagement.

Indeed.

Mar Vista 5/06/02

John Thomas, He Had a Hammer – *May 2002*

I swing my John Thomas lunch pail in my right hand
it makes me want to break loose
it makes me need and want to sing
I carry my John Thomas records in my blood
they allow me to mingle with the ongoing traffic of i think i know you
the vocal mountain range of John Thomas' mind at work
full of all night, and every which way, and yes sir
early morning, almost one
Sunday
s. a. calls and says John Thomas is gone
he helmed the raft baby
he sang the lighting here
and did he dance
he danced up and down every set of stairs you could toss his way
like Anthony Quinn in Lawrence of Arabia
John was and is a river to his people
he was the eighth dwarf, the fourth musketeer, the fourteenth day of
Dracula, the magnificent eighth...
make me want to break loose
make me want and need to sing
early morning, almost one
Sunday
he be the light here
he be the dance

3/31/0

Border of Boredom – *April 2000*

The phone coughed up blood when it heard you speak
The militia can't find the aliens in your soul
Some lonely patient swears by your cold
I wanted to go skating but the world was too huge
I sit in coffee some months beyond, some tones old
Rattle the illegal bones, shake up the orbit and grin
The takers and the took, they all love to sing
The cut up, the pristine, they all share the taxi ride
A howling season climbs aboard the ear
Take me sailing, take me whole
Come along and say your sooth
Ebb and flow, debutantes and vermouth, traffic is
opening its heart to allow us to glow
The border of boredom is on fire
The international house of pain is having
a closeout sale
The country is in my underwear
The universe you claim is in the way you roll
Christ, baby, I could get behind you
if the universe you ride
would learn to dance just
a little bit slow

7/7/99

This poem also was published in Little Red Book #25,
***Nomads of Oblivion**.*

Rambler, American – *February 2000*

The clouds were on the dance floor last night when I heard the room move and ask me for a date. I thought maybe I had enough names on guest list of good morning. I thought I could move through traffic without being caught. You sit around the rose garden even if all the roses have risen and run away, you sit around and wonder if the impresario is going to kiss you once, twice or all year long, that's a helluva lot kisses, and the moving men come and their backs are hurting, they look at you as if you were a young pretty notion running wild across the Irish heather, yes, and the clouds were on the dance floor last night when the government came to take me back.

Unknown

The Unknown Bukowski Thriller – *August 1999*

Hot seedy afternoon Los Angeles do what you do or die type of ambience. Bukowski holds a cold one against his forehead as a young ingénue (female) and her escort (not female) enter his office.

Are you a private dick? She asks, and Bukowski opens his portfolio, examines young pictures of himself, nods back to her.

Private enough. How can I solve your problem?

This guy alongside me claims he wants to be a poet. I heard you could make it feasible for him to do just that.

I do so very much want to become a poet, the escort chimes in. We hear broken glass, screams, yelling off screen. Bukowski opens the cold one. Time to move on beyond just holding it against the forehead.

Kid, nothing I can say will make you a poet. Either you got it or you don't.

Don't say that to me, Bukowski. My Dracula friends say you are hep.

If being a survivor means you're hep, maybe... Shut your eyes.

What, Bukowski? Why should I shut my eyes?

Shut your goddamn eyes, kid.

The escort follows suit.

What do you see in your heart, kid? Or head, if you must. See something in there?

It's kind of cloudy, Bukowski. I don't see so good this early in the day.

He's a night person, the lady grins.

Not good enough, kid. You must be able to see shit anytime of the day or night. You can't just see things when you want to.

Do you see things anytime you shut your eyes? The lady asks, slowly caressing Bukowski's desk.

Do you like caressing my desk?

I think I'm seeing something now, Bukowski, the escort laughs. I don't know what it is, actually, but I think I just might be beginning to see it.

Go somewhere and put words around it. Go somewhere and hum a tune. Go someplace and sing.

I can't sing too well, Bukowski.

I don't give a damn. Sing anyway. Poetry is song. Song is whatever it is that gets you singing.

I don't know about all this, Bukowski. I don't think I'm cut out for this.

The escort shrivels up in a corner of the office. The ingénue takes Bukowski's beer and slurps it.

Maybe you're seeing something he tells her.

Maybe I am, she tells him.

The heat bounces up and down. The heat is everywhere. The heat is seeing everyone. The heat is a lover. This is a love story about a poet. Who saw everything. And then some.

He sang very damn good.

He sang all day. He sang all night.

He's singing somewhere right now.

7/16/99

The road that takes you – *January/February 2004*

The displaced, the dispossessed, the disinherited, they
all come to hear the new disc that claims love
will get out of jail in time to come to the
swearing in of the new world. Love slipped its disk
and the doctors are in closed door session
trying to placate the cure that may or may not
come home in time for the new world's christening.
When the lights fade, when the vocabulary dismantles
itself, we are deciphering grunts and sighs that
illuminate the new world's dictionary.
Bear all you can, and if you break, let me
hand you some double sticky tape to patch you
up long enough to make the next bus
due any second.
Hold a candle up to the road that takes you,
hold it so you don't burn your fingers.
I didn't build the road that tries to take me,
but I can take whatever it wants my feet
to feel. Walk with focus, stumble with verve,
the ever deepening holes raise their hands
and sweet talk our destination to stop
trying to get us home. The ever deepening
wound promises it will relax. Can I trust
it when it sings this way to me? Have I
truly been enticed again into putting my foot
into a trap? When the lights fade, when
the language disintegrates, can I hold you
close to me. The road says it will take us
to the good time coming. We synchronize our
watches and time goes on strike. Close now,
we hold. Our own. The next bus is due
any second.

West L. A.

Earth Fell Hard – *April 2002*

Earth fell hard out of bed
and the books of love implode
as we grope our way through
forests of angry rhythm. Lovers, though,
somersault across the abyss
can the music actually dissolve so well it will never
show up again in the bloodstream
of the moment? Sway, then, let your eyes
rise toward the long and tall afternoon
of tired skin and angry bone

Sheree Rose

somehow ascending the fire
toward some ways and means of the spirit
that still can hum the radiant
language of hope. Earth tore itself up and
screamed Save Me and the large editors
wrote small print volumes of expertise
to heal Earth's pain. Save Me, the sun
wrote in its autobiography, don't let me burn
you up to much. Dear Human, can you
play that sweet ongoing depot of a sound? Can
you hootenanny latitude and longitude? The
torn face of hello puts its history back
together and there is a music that refuses
to crawl into a corner and shrivel up.
Sway, then, my fellow lovers, let your
eyes rise toward the long and tall
glass of empathy. Save Me, the Earth
screams, kicking at anyone that tries,
Save Me, and you pick up your heart which
is sound, and you begin to wail and row
your spirit's canoe downriver toward
the ocean of love. Sway, then, to the
unheard symphony. There is a yodel in every tree
there is a place to land in every dream and
the houses of hate suck themselves into
bottomless holes and never come again to
interrupt the soiree of who we are.
Dear Humans, can you play that sweet ongoing
sound? Can you?

9/13/01

In the House of Warren Oates – *October 2002*

Let's be honest, the only thing that really makes me search for film is the character actor. Leads? Stars? Whatever they may one day turn out to be...well, maybe so, more so maybe not...one of the reasons I sought out Dwight Yokem's South of Heaven, North of Hell or whatever the handle of it was...wasn't so much for Dwight or Bridget Fonda...but because Luke Askew was in it. That is also what sent me out to Bill Paxton's directing debut, Frailty...the one with Matthew McConnaughey and Powers Booth...and Bill himself. Luke Askew appeared in some of the most influential films of the sixties, Easy Rider, Cool Hand Luke... then later appeared in diverse ditties such as Great Northfield Minnesota Raid, The Green Berets, The devil's Brigade, Flareup, Culpepper Cattle Company, Monte Walsh, Walking Tall Part Two, The Beast Within, some futuristic mumbo jumbo fantasy sword doohickey with David Carradine, I believe...Attack on Terror: FBI vs. the Klan, a TV thing, which had him in a large scary part as a redneck killer...he starred in an obscure Canadian film called Slipstream, i believe his only starring part...well it goes on, but that is why i go to the movies, the character folks, they draw me in...oh yes, Luke actually walked me up to my door one night, i had the pleasant experience of doing some beers with him and Mills Watson, another fine character fellow who is in Oregon now cause the parts just weren't here/there...

I called this rap the house of Warren Oates, and here I am going on and on about Luke, but it's a wide circle of dancers, the Dwight film also had Matt Clark and Bo Hopkins, and these guys worked a lot in the sixties, seventies, and then it all sort of got sparse in the eighties and nineties...

The house of Warren Oates is an undying house. Tonight I was in, for the first time, the Two Lane Blacktop room of the house. The room had been built by Monte Hellman. Monte and Warren did a number of rooms together. The Shooting, Ride in the Whirlwind, Cockfighter (from the Charles Willeford novel).

A sparse road film epic with Warren, James Taylor, Dennis Wilson,

Laurie Bird, Alan Vint...Warren Oates actually got solid billing in a Best Film of the Year thing back in the sixties...Do you folks out there know it? Warren Oates was in Ride the High Country and he wouldn't take a bath until his brothers dragged him into the water trough. Warren Oates starred in the ill fated Chandler(had another title at one point)with Leslie Caron. This item was disowned by the filmmaker(s), they claimed Studio Boss James Aubrey butchered their film in the cutting room. A mess, this turned out to be. Warren Oates unnerved me in an Outer Limits episode. Warren Oates went to Mexico looking finally for Alfredo Garcia's head. Warren Oates was in Stripes with Bill Murray.

The house of Warren Oates is large, and enriching, and ongoing whenever his rooms cross your eyesight. He and Rip Torn appeared in a low budget action adventure deal set off the Carolinas. Neville Brand also wound up in it. Now, can you name it? James Mason was the actual lead. Odd cast, you say? Rock it on, baby.

The character actor is the spine and backbone and backbeat of all of this work. Don't care who the lead or star is. Without the character actor, you got no character, and without the behavior of characters, you got nothing to sing to me about.

David Straithairn's repeated "Help, help in the building" at the end of John Sayles' City of Hope, is more profound, and mind shattering than all the special effects you can hope to ever assemble.

But I wax on...When Charles McGraw's vindictive killer steps out of the John Alton L.A. shadows in T-Men(Anthony Mann)my roller coaster heart plummets, plunges, and zooms.

Be well now. Have fun watching those character actors.

Mar Vista, CA

REVIEWS – *July 2001*

Doghouse Roses by Steve Earle
Houghton Mifflin $22.00
Eclectic songwriter Steve Earle makes his strong debut in the world of fiction with this collection of short stories. His range is wide and heartfelt, and works on many levels. His subjects range from Texas musicians trying to find a place called home, to Vietnamese officers dying of cancer looking for a quicker honorable death. There is even room for a quiet yet haunting look at an aging radical feminist in Europe exploring her past through a young American. And then there is my favorite, The Red Suitcase, about how a man used to his routine is disturbingly changed forever by the lack of experience of a new deputy in town. These stories are accessible, radiate the human condition, and are a welcome debut to the fiction dancefloor from an artist who has proven his storytelling ability in the music genre.

The Cold Six Thousand by James Ellroy
Knopf $26.95
Demon dog Ellroy's first novel since American Tabloid, and a more than worthy sequel to that sprawling novel that dealt with American malaise. This one picks up with a roar and accelerates past all ideas of a finish line. Opening with the John Kennedy Dallas assassination, it culminates years later in the murders of Martin Luther King and Robert Kennedy. This one, as usual for Ellroy, bops, slams, hums, kicks, groans, shoots straight and then through you, and ends with one of the most vicious comeuppances ever in the world of fiction. If you follow the Ellroy river, this baby is a fine way to get wet and then some.

Rides of the Midway by Lee Durkee
Norton $25.95
A quiet yet full account of coming of age in the South. Told

from the point of view of a young man who is angry yet empathetic to the holes in the streets of the fabric of the world, Durkee's assured style is both surreal and rooted in the meat and potatoes now. Not ever overwritten, it does take chances, and goes into corners you might not have felt were there. An effortless first novel that enrichingly shines through its character's experiences, and encompasses the bones and skin of all its people with a storyteller's eye.

April 1865.The Month That Saved America by Jay Winik Harper Collins $32.50
A beautiful Civil War history that reads like quality fiction. Winik's research, and presentation keeps the reader turning the pages and experiencing Robert E. Lee and Grant, and all else concerned, as never before. Enriching on every page, and the kind of history that just walks into your soul and takes root there. A momentous month in our past, and a momentous account of that month, in which many things could have gone many different ways from the way they turned out. A must read.

Language from the bottom of the six pack of maybe – *November 2000*

Al Gore and George Bush dropped in through the chimney and went through my ice box looking for incriminating finger food. You guys didn't bring Nader or Buchanan or anyone else with you, I asked. They both shrugged it off, arm wrestled in front of my digital cable hookup, and began singing songs about poets they never read but heard were somewhat decent. You guys like Gerald Locklin? I asked. I mean, if one of you guys could quote me some Locklin, I might consider casting my vote for you. Both candidates gave me spaced out looks and I knew it was a lost cause. Get out of my way, I want to watch Forrest Tucker on the Encore Western Station. We like Forrest Tucker, both of them said in unison. Yeah, that's not going to wash, you guys let me down when I asked for a bit of Locklin. Nader could do Locklin, I bet. On my Encore Western station Tucker was building the Rock Island Line and Adrian Booth was supposedly a big shot Indian woman, and Bruce Cabot was the villain, the same Bruce Cabot that saved Fay Wray on Skull Island in King Kong. You got any home grown, Mr. Wannberg? Bush asked. Can I borrow a bunch of your videos? Gore asked. We can go and learn Locklin, they both said, getting on their knees. Please, please, vote for us. The Rock Island Trail jumped out of my TV and entered both Bush and Gore and impaled them on their spikes. Gee, this digital cable stuff is kind of dramatic, I felt. I called up my cable company, which now goes by the name of AT and T Broadband. Yeah, I'm afraid my Republic western was so interactive, the railroad leapt out of my screen and impaled the two top candidates for president. Could you send a guy out to un-impale them. Yes, the cable guy said, and began quoting Gerald Locklin. The world was and is still alive.

from the bottom of the cigar box to the
heart of the moment

Charles Bukowski, Mountain Man – *August 2000*

(from the pages of Americana, a new hero is born)

The immigrant wagon train is headed West toward the promised land of poetry and sun. Despite the dangers of hostile Indians and renegade outlaws, they are determined to make a new start.

"We need someone to guide us," the immigrant leader says to his colleagues. "We need a mountain man to get us West. A guide, a friend, a seer, a true hero."

"Then you need Bukowski," says one of the locals, on his way for a morning libation. "Bukowski's your man. Fighter, lover, hunter, singer..."

Bukowski saunters out of the local saloon. His face has a lived through look. The immigrants come to him, moths drawn to a flame of life.

"Bukowski man," says the leader, "could you guide us to the promised land of poetry and sun?"

"The poetry is in you already, but the sun, well, when the clouds part, you just feel it. But I could stand to go out West. Land around here is getting crowded with speculators and I hate speculators. I spit on them. You got any pretty women in your immigrant train, fellow?"

"Our women are exemplary," says one of the elders.

"We'll find out just how much," says Bukowski. "You boys could go on in the saloon and settle my tab."

Later, that same month. On the trail. Bukowski single handedly bests a band of desperadoes with his fists. The desperado leader, his life ebbing on the ground, is in awe of Bukowski's prowess.

"Muy macho, mister," he says, "you must be some kind of a poet."

"Yeah, well, some days it pays. Some days you wonder."

Later, that same week. Bukowski is dealing with some Indians to allow the immigrants through their land.

"These pilgrims don't want to take the gold out of your land, Indians. I myself could use a little gold, for my teeth, mind you. But I respect your rap about the land and such and won't mess around with your way of looking and such, and hearing."

"You smoke the pipe with us, Bukowski," the Indian leader says.

"I think I'd rather drink some of your merriment stuff, hoss. That pipe stuff sort of gets me too introspective for my own good, if you get the drift."

Later, that same decade. A young wisp of an immigrant gal and Bukowski are sharing a tender moment by a serene sort of creek.

"Your words make my ventricles throb, Bukowski," the wisp says.

"I'm too old for you, virgin lady. Plus aren't you spoken for to one of the younger elders. Or older youngers."

"I could let down my hair, Bukowski, for a man of life such as you are."

"I'm too much a loner, a fighter, a wanderer. I couldn't be still long enough to give you what you need."

"I need your six gun, Bukowski. The way it smokes."
"Don't let the light blind you, lady."

We see the new home of the immigrant train. The immigrants bow down, they kiss the earth.

"You got us to our home, mountain man. We are forever in your debt. How can we repay you?"

"Get me some beer. Buy some of my words."

"We will make poet laureate of our new found colony."

"In a true democracy, friend, there is no room for a poet laureate. Just get me some beer."

A young scrub hands Bukowski a barrel of beer.

"Thanks, young scrub," Bukowski says, downing the barrel in one gulp.

"Gee, Mr. Bukowski, you got powerful lungs."

"It comes from singing with the coyotes, boy," Bukowski nods, belching, farting.

That night around the camp fire the immigrant hootenanny band sings this ditty:

Charles Bukowski is a man
Yes a big man
he fought for all poets and immigrants
to keep all poets and immigrants free
Charles Bukowski is a man
yes a big man
he sings all his songs
to keep you and me free

"Well, Bukowski, what will you do now?" the immigrant leader asks.

Bukowski says, "roam the earth. Fight the good fight. Drink the good drink. What else can I do?"

"Stay with us, Bukowski. Build a house. Tend the land," says the immigrant leader.

"I'm a wandering star, friend. Just a roustabout and a dancing man," says Bukowski.

Bukowski begins to dance... we fade out slowly.

5/20/2000

Review – *December 1999*

Scar Tissue by A. D. Winans
Little Red Book series #6 $5
Lummox Press, POB 5301, San Pedro, CA 90733

The poet is a sum of him or her historical memories, Father, Mother, the war of life, the way the shrapnel of living lands and infects the skin, to be hummed years later as you go through the airport inspection line of memory.

A.D. Winans knows that the B-side of Wound is Learning. One pays attention to the scars. The roots therein produce new foliage of empathy.

This is Winans' Blues. The years of being child, son of Mother and Father, the witness to the war of men and women, of man and man, of life, and from such a witness, the ability to sing the past back up, in order to embrace the precarious present.

The skin needs replenishing, needs sun, air, rapport, or it shrivels. The dance demands you retain some fleeting scrap of music so you can move; this courageous exploration into one's family history, past, locked closet of personal pain, becomes finally, an illumination, an embrace, a landing of rattling pieces of human into some cohesive bloodstream of love.

The Scar Tissue of A.D. Winans has produced fertile earth of possibility, hope and awareness.

SCOTT WANNBERG

RANT #1 – *Date unknown*

The clouds were on the dance floor last night when I heard the room move and ask me for a date. I thought maybe I had enough names on guest list of good morning. I thought I could move through traffic without being caught. You sit around the rose garden even if all the roses have risen and run away, you sit around and wonder if the impresario is going to kiss you once, twice or all year long, that's a helluva lot kisses, and the moving men come and their backs are hurting, they look at you as if you were a young pretty notion running wild across the Irish heather, yes, and the clouds were on the dance floor last night when the government came to take me back.

The Carma Bums, 1992,
photo by Jay Green,
altered by S.A. Griffin

Scarecrow – *January 1999*

Sherrise Iverson and Matthew Shepard
hand me the songbooks of love.
Get the words right when you roar out loud
I wanted to find the right kind of food
to match the hope fighting to stay alive
inside the hunger. Turn to your right,
dream a little left. The city on the hill
is made of mud. The city on the hill won't know your name
unless you belt it out
with all your pain, empathy, and belief.
The antihomosexual gang outside Matthew Shepard's
funeral this afternoon waved signs that
said He Is Going To Hell.
Hell, though, being right here on Earth,
was not filled with anyone but them.
Hell, being right here, is the residence Jeffrey
Strohmeier lives in when he tells me over my TV imagery
that everyone is to blame for Sherrise but him.
A lot of people were able to fit in that
Stateline women's bathroom according to such a theory.
Match that hope trying to stay alive in your hunger.
Listen to the bruised airline of burning
it crashes repeatedly in the name of hate
and hate's natural father and mother, fear.
The poor biker who discovered Shepard in a coma
tied to a fence said he looked at first like a Scarecrow
and scarecrows are easy to burn down into amnesia
and hate's natural mother and father want you to donate
money and time to the future
the orchestra of fist, the aria of bludgeon, the rhythm

and blues of strangulation, ah, the air is opening
to allow the air to enter, the air is thinning out now, just
like the crowd, and alone
we stumble up the trail toward the welcome home of hope.
Shepard beaten so hard they could see brain stem
subzero dancehall of large quiet sky
much larger than the claustrophobic end game
Strohmeier gave Sherrise
can the bag of empathy hold?
Can the game be called on account of dark?
Scarecrows are easy to tear apart in this resumé of
crow
less
faith
Those antihomosexual folks at Shepard's funeral
called him a Sodomite and because of that he deserved
a life in Hell, whatever Hell other than this one
at times could be
Those antihomosexual folks with their predictable one note
rage
have committed a much darker offense
They haven't fucked anyone in the ass
but they have fucked all believers of empathy and tolerance
in the heart
and as you know from your medical journals
a hole in the heart is a hard one to come in out
of the rain from
It snowed in casper this afternoon
as Matthew Shepard got placed
his two killers, both young, await their dance card in jail

rumors abound that one of them has already said
he deserves to die
Strohmeier in Nevada told me David Cash his pal was a bad man
and a horrible human
David Cash is currently enrolled in Berkeley
getting a degree in something certainly not Feeling
The federal government sent down one of their "gay"
representatives to the funeral in Casper
One hell of a job description, that, "gay" representative
Turn around now. Grab the one you love. Grab yourself
if you don't love anyone.
Turn around now and show me how you can move to the unheard
music. Turn around
and show me the shape of the country you live in, and through.
Sing one for Sherrise Iverson
Sing one for Matthew Shepard
Sing one for Jeffrey Strohmeier who just realized his friend
David Cash was not a good friend
Sing one for david Cash who may run into himself one day but I doubt it
Sing one for those two guys in Wyoming who tore Matthew
Shepard apart for no reason
You never need a reason to show how easy you can tear something apart
Sing one for me
Sing one for you
Keep singing when the lights go down
We'll make a record
It'll be swell

We'll make a damn fine record
Sing one for Sherrise Iverson's daddy
who was too busy gambling
to make sure she was okay
Casinos are made, of course, for little children
Sing one for those antihomosexual assholes
who just had to come to shepard's funeral
to send him off in their own empathetic style
They fuck my heart still
They fuck my heart so bad I can't ever ask them back
We all make such a damn fine sound
Sherries Iverson and Matthew Shepard give us our sheet music
Sing my friend and
sing like you've never sung one before
You got a damn wonderful voice

10/16/98

Also published in Little Red Book #3 **Equal Opportunity Sledgehammer** *1999*

bucketful of yes – *"All Poetry Issue" April 1999*

hold the earth in your hand today
the circus is moving into your bedroom
all the animals are gold
the government finally on hiatus
not likely to return for years
when the armies implode
no war tonight on the dinner table
excited hair murmurs of wind
sleep easy guarding the door
nobody irritable is due soon
  hold your own in the ongoing investigation
  tap your favorite tune with your toes
  they'll be coming around soon enough
    with gossip and drugs to ease the pain
    it won't be for some time though
and the dancefloor has just opened up a bank account in your heart
  no dying needed tonight on the table
    all the animals let you into their cages
      they recognize the school you came out of
        they love the cut of your soul

5/10/98
Scott Wannberg

Also published in Little Red Book #3 ***Equal Opportunity Sledgehammer*** *1999*

The LITTLE RED BOOK Series

A Note About the Titles

When I told Scott I wanted to do a chapbook of his poetry but I didn't know what to call it, he came up with these ideas:

Listerine Kill
Jimmy Hoffa lives in My Underwear
The Timothy Leary 2-step Debacle
Rye Krisp from Hell
Zen Amnesia
Strobe-light Stomach Trouble
Resonant Psychosis
English Muffin Death Trap
Crispy Critters Squirm for Love
Hard Artery
Sputnik of Death
Chuck Steak, American Hero
Esmeralda & Quasimodo Unchained
Lucifer's Navel
Strom Thurmond Ate My Homework

How we ended up with **Equal Opportunity Sledgehammer** *&* **Nomads of Oblivion**, *I can't say (mostly because I can't remember that far back), but Scott's mind was as agile as Nijinsky, as you will see in the following poetry.*

Equal Opportunity Sledgehammer LRB # 3 – 1999

Introduction

Scott Wannberg is an alphabet magician
with a thirst for long tall glasses
of imagery and chords
he has the cinema on his elbow

politics on his larynx
surreality on the back of his knee
he sings into the history and marrow of
Planet Vibrant
with the laughter and pain that lives side
by side
in the heart's kaleidoscope
he names the constellations
with one vowel tied behind his back
he escapes the barrel before it drops over
Niagara
and he tells us what he sees with the water
of Lourdes
rising like a Phoenix from the ashes
like a New Mexico from the embers
like a bird with a beak full of memory
he flies ever near like the crop duster
in North By Northwest
kicking up this culture's particles
in a cameo of suspense that looks like love

Ellyn Maybe

get stuff

you get stuff to make you invulnerable
around ten at night
when the sky looks crooked
under the moody light
the kids arranged for you
so you could see yourself
running   scared
as the sweat of the nation
becomes a new ocean
that only a navigator
such as yourself
could handle
you get stuff to ward off
suffering and
it comes in a tube that
is blessed by all the larger than not
religious organizations
perhaps you bumped up against   one
on the rapid transit
when the sun beat down
on the roof
keeping its own peculiar time
get stuff is what the adverting agency
working out of a stalled camaro
in front of my building
sings
whenever i run out
to become one with non nature
we are nothing but stuff
pretending to be more enriched than need be
perhaps you rode the perfect wave
in your head
the sea that morning
agreed with you

the war held up by traffic
time for once
to enjoy the music
that   may or may not be there
but it never stops you
from hearing it anyhow

8/10/97

Raindog

come along and take time to hear this tune
for dave gans

the light got shot out by somebody who claimed
they knew the hit tune
the light took a vacation and we stumbled
around in the lack of it
looking for the good food and the city
that claimed it loved music
you remember that city?
it grew out of our skin one inevitable summer
when tears became rivers and the
men and women who swam there ail
danced so well
the government chased itself because it
                            claimed it was bored
                            it needed a job
i was walking sideways in a one way room
and all the movies i grew up with
ran backward
and talked odd
there are days and hours and times when
you want to pull out your hair and then
get maybe mistook for somebody with something to
say
there are hours in which the escalators don't
go anywhere but the place you don't need to go
okay enough by me for sure
my bones go cantankerous my bones go silly
into the ongoing breath of the day
i listen for the rhythm i listen for the sway
put both feet up and place both feet down
to the ongoing dancefloor of the wounded earth
learning to sing
i wart for people on my t.v. to become sort of alive
and do what they claim they can
it never happens
i shut it off and go sailing in my blood
to the music of who we can be

if we'd only listen and move to the sound
of that incorrigible empathy that wondrous
epiphany
Dave Cans was dancing across the ongoing
ocean's floor
he was singing and writing new cities of
yes
I heard him yodeling
I heard him snapping his mind and creating new
canyons in which you could
go humming
on your day off
come on and move to the sound then
come on and flow to the moment of who you can be
come on and tap it out a bit
the peculiar music that parts your hair
and lets you roar
the world is mad the world needs to get a job
the world sits outside with an uzi
demanding we crawl
no way
the music won't let us
it widens our brain
it broils our heart
the heart is writing a memoir
the road is sleeping it off
a long night a long year a long second
come on and take off your shoes and fly to
any moon that finds you
Dave Cans was singing
and the sky nodded its head
Dave Cans is singing
and the light is working fine
Dave Cans is singing
and the human light is smiling wide

4/13/96

when i fall to pieces

let your dinner set awhile
tell me about your children
the ones with mountains in their hair
i hear the cold walking soft
down the hail to the room
where music used to sign its name
there is no final parting
we all go lonely to the dance
when i fall to pieces
will you sweep me up in a dreaming dustbin
i hear myself
hearing the cries and whispers
of vulnerable heroes and heroines
who stayed a little too long
they meant to get home in time
but the traffic was too hard
when i become one with the missing
will you count on me to show up
for your better behavior
the sad refrains open up bank accounts
in firm rooms and
the lighting there is very smooth
i hear myself sometimes
wondering if 1 wonder too much
about the bewilderment in the drinking water
all this angst makes me lazy
i need to get home
before the falling arch
hear then the cries
believe in the whispers
of those fools who are my loved
they stayed too long
they never knew
that there is nothing

right or wrong
the whole damn menu
was full of food
that couldn't possibly go down
when you see me
bleeding freely
i want to ask you
to come on down
there used to be
some kind of love
now i hear the cannons
they say your name
so well
i fall to pieces
i used to over reach
now the top is the new bottom
let me wonder no more
the crty streets are breathing deep
their doctor is a fine looking
way to go
the whole damn city
has a headache
i fall to pieces
when i hear the earth
sing

4/26/98

dedicated

when i had a skin that could last more than an hour
i could dance the dark side of the
uncontrolled tower; whimsical men and their
supportive women are gathering as my bones
argue with the sun;
i wanted to win this big one just for you baby
lay me down in the silent aisle
dedicated to everyone who sold so well the
sustaining image of just what we wanted to die trying
to live up to
tell my lady i wanted to fly the soft route
in the hard to digest hearing aid
the minutes beckon
i am just one more ornery man
standing in a line that never ends
or begins
dark homicidal food carts full of
good resumes
stand at the side
of the big event
that is our bloodstream
learning to sing
dedicated to all who laughed the loudest
as sunrise cut through the smoke
and addressed our naked sin
with jazz that would save us
that would name us
you claimed you were above being named
by anything resembling music
yet you tremble when the soothsaying
overdubs come crashing down on your
goodtime afternoon skin
i didnt want to overstay my youth
in the troubled times of love

say what you want
aim what you mean
the small cafes are crowded with
hungry cab drivers
they have driven all night
to get us to this place of
compensation
they have torn the earth in
shreds to
name the new high school
where we never graduate for real
yet we look so damn good
in those sweaters of
hope

4/26/98

Kick it

the habits a man and a woman wrap themselves in as if
invisible is an easily accessed code
hear them at work now in the alley
any alley
the one you claim doesn't exist
inside your spacious looking face
in a town where nobody wears a watch
time says gnarly things behind your back
hear the lovers cleaning their guns
at work now in any language that will keep them afloat
the times are argumentably dark lately
i know they give out precarious flashlights at the
border
with instructions manuals on how to somehow behave
yes, well, good enough for some, maybe
the habitual remains of a man and a woman
everywhere you bump
excuse anything you can find time for
get connected
kick in and find yourself in high gear
the fire is out of control
the fire is what you always wanted for Christmas
hear the lovers becoming one now
as the explosion goes off
so loud you will never have to hear
fear
calling your name
again

12/3/98

sure things come in all sizes

                ornery humans again doing stupid
things
to each other
      lovely vulnerable idiots
creating sure things
        of all sizes
around the next corner
Utopia waits
        for a light
inhale the new sky
the melodic town of air inside
      law abiding heart attacks
retroactive love affairs
      piling high in the southwest corner
near the only working heater
      saw an ambidextrous enough fellow
tap dancing through a minefield
he said he was on his way to the show
i checked the schedule but none was listed
think you might have the wrong season, i said
      it's a sure thing, son, he said
and his nouns and verbs got tangled in barbed wire
he danced good though
i couldn't hold that against his bad timing
      and now the moon is disappearing
as the car hops get ready to wail
Utopia sits in a corner water hole
nursing a tall slow dream
      the bones inside our skin shake rattle hum
maybe someday soon even roll
      behave yourself now
get yourself a tv series

teach the headlines to hear your story right
      men and women living alone
in the luxury hotel of unable to talk
men and women who ask me for a dime a date a
history
      ran into a not so sure thing in the lobby
it recognized me from years ago
reached into my pocket and pulled out
some kind of subject matter that
could prevail in the long run
      see you somewhere where the pain is soft
      see you in the affirmation tank
      the one down at the end of the aisle
      that goes on too long
do you practice the love?
do you rinse the windows of faith
at least twice a month?
      sure things waiting for you in the parking lot
armed to the inevitable tooth
grab your bulletproof face
hold up your shield of i am indeed what i guess i
ought to be
      the night is just getting out of bed
      the night asks you to give it enough time
          to put on its shoes
the right way
      do you endorse the fire?
      well, hell, the fire endorses me
      and we got home about the same time
      as the sure things turned to wine
      as all sure things eventually
      evaporate and are eaten by time

5/10/98

fractures make the heart grow fonder

      the mighty all encompassing dice
just fell hard on my head
   all the sharp angles are now waving me
haphazardly on
   toward some uncontrollable circus
of the banshee soul
   where nothing is ever forgot
except memory
   in the soft shoe hall of the so-called invulnerable
children
   your foot hits a new low
which is just another new country
of lost dancers asking you for a light
you make the effort to go deep into your pockets
any pockets
   come on, baby, the earth says when you
show up for the loan
come on, baby, let's see what you're made of
wind and tunnels full of dark
   skin that won't last the night
      come on baby, i heard an owl say to a mouse
fractures make the heart grow fonder
in this white sale of maybe i can help you out after all
in this new season of wary skateboards that aren't
what
they claim to be

    you go through all the brochures looking for the one
marked Stay Here and Do Not Go Further
      the one with the house in it that will
never turn you away
      no matter what weather arrives
claiming it knows you so well,
   no one ever knows anyone
    that well
come on, baby, the arresting officer said to the
running away evening
   show me where your hair hangs
     show me where your world learned to dance
    come on, baby, the morning said to
the bone collector
   let me hear you shake it
     let me hear you feel it
       let me hear.

12/6/98

had to know

the phones broke their promise
they always swore they'd work for us
had to know the result
tried to get through
static said its name everywhere
i didn't really need to know such things
the poets are insane, the government warned
metaphors such anyhow
had to know the outcome of
the mystery
a car got sent for us
we didn't fit in it very well
the circus has enough room for us
they always swore they'd be there for
us
which one of us is the down?
who walks the high wire and gets home dean?
had to know the name of the new game
came with every good intention
reached into my one carry on bag
seemed there was a hole in the bottom
a long enough way down to go
tried to angle in
got hooked by angelic bait
the long road home has no parole officer
come and whisper your home's real address
the tender sky goes in for night
its mother has been yelling for days

4/15/98

Dead Lover Canyon

the Muse broke prison about 3:10 am
yesterday and
all the townsfolk are perturbed
and sweating a little more
profuse
I would of joined In with the posse
but my heart just couldn't take
the strain
Got to stay here with my legs propped up
remembering all the loves I
took barefoot down to
Dead Lover Canyon
you know, the 8th or 9th
blunder of the world
where you can only see the sky
when your mind goes to sleep
the trouble with the damn mind
is that it never wants to
let you take a restI sit here in the dark
the coyotes are singing on key
I hear a miracle is going to show any day
I hear a miracle is going to run for president
even just might win
a few counties or so

1/29/95

The Experiment

the experiment wrote us up in its notebook
did we pass the test?
which one of us is the good person?
the sound of war goes on and on
unrepentant, boring, excruciating
the lovers finally arrive
they seem to live up to their potential
the experiment has a twin brother
in some mental hospital
that was built by a passionate
architect who later hung himself
nobody hangs themselves around here
the rope is very weak
soon i will get to make a speech
to a large serious group of people
who claim they might be my friends
i hope i don't fail
them
failure is not something one tolerates
here
the experiment does not like it very much
if you fall
you get taken out back into the dark
and for a long time
no one ever sees or hears you
i like being seen and heard
even if i have nothing to say
the experiment loves us when we have nothing
to say
it smiles and kisses us and
the future, whatever that is,
is encouraging, and rhythmic.

10/18/98

bucketful of yes

hold the earth in your hand today
the circus is moving into your bedroom
all the animals are gold
the government finally on hiatus
not likely to return for years
bucketfuls of yes falling on your skin
remember to weep in tune
when the armies implode
no war tonight on the dinner table
excited hair and murmurs of wind
sleep easy guarding the door
nobody irritable is due too soon
   hold your own in the ongoing investigation
   tap your favorite tune with your toes
   they'll be coming around soon enough
   with gossip and drugs to ease the pain
     it won't be for some time though
and the dancefloor has just opened up a bank account
in your heart
     no dying needed tonight on the table
        all the animals let you into their cages
           they recognize the school you came out of
          they love the cut of your soul

5/10/98

Scarecrow

Sherrise Iverson and Matthew Shepard
hand me the songbooks of love.
Get the words right when you roar out loud
I wanted to find the right kind of food
to match the hope fighting to stay alive
inside the hunger. Turn to your right,
Dream a little left. The city on the hill
is made of mud. The city on the hill won't know your
name
unless you belt it out
with all your pain, empathy, and belief.
The antihomosexual gang outside Matthew Shepard's
funeral this afternoon waved signs that
said He Is Going To Hell.
Hell, though, being right here, on Earth,
was not filled with anyone but them.
Hell, being right here, is the residence Jeremy
Strohmeier lives in when he tells me over my TV
imagery
that everyone is to blame for Sherrise but him.
A lot of people were able to fit in that
Stateline women's bathroom according to such a
theory.
Match that hope trying to stay alive in your hunger.
Listen to the bruised airline of burning
it crashes repeatedly in the name of hate
and hate's natural father and mother, fear.
The poor biker who discovered Shepard in a coma
tied to a fence said he looked at first like a Scarecrow
and scarecrows are easy to bum down into amnesia
and hate's natural mother and father want you to
donate
money and time to the future
the orchestra of fist, the aria of bludgeon, the rhythm

and blues of strangulation, ah, the air is opening
to allow the air to enter, the air is thinning out now, just
like the crowd, and alone
we stumble up the trail toward the welcome home of
hope.
Shepard beaten so hard they could see brain stem
subzero dancehall of large quiet sky
much larger than the claustrophobic end game
Strohmeier gave Sherrise
can the bag of empathy hold on?
can the game be called on account of dark?
Scarecrows are easy to tear apart in this resumé of
crow
less
faith
Those antihomosexual folks at Shepard's funeral
called him a Sodomite and because of that he
deserved
a life in Hell, whatever Hell other than this one
at times could be
Those antihomosexual folks with their predictable one
note
rage
have committed a much darker larger offense
They haven't fucked anyone in the ass
but they have fucked all believers of empathy and
tolerance
in the heart
and as you know from your medical journals
a hole through the heart is a hard one to come in out
of the rain from
It snowed in Casper this afternoon
as Matthew Shepard got placed
his two killers, both young, await their dance card

in jail
rumors abound that one of them has already said
he deserves to die
Strohmeier in Nevada told me David Cash his pal was
a bad
man and a horrible human
David Cash is currently enrolled in Berkeley
getting a degree in something
certainly not Feeling
The federal government sent down one of their "gay"
representatives to the funeral in Casper
One hell of a job description, that, "gay representative
Turn around now. Grab the one you love. Grab yourself
if you don't love anyone.
Turn around now and show me how you can move to
the unheard
music. Turn around
and show me the shape of the country you live in, and
through.
Sing one for Sherrise Iverson
Sing one for Matthew Shepard
Sing one for Jeremy Strohmeier who just realized his
friend
David Cash was not a good friend
Sing one for David Cash who may run into himself one
day
but I doubt it
Sing one for those two guys in Wyoming who tore
Matthew
Shepard apart for no reason
You never need a reason to show how easy
you can tear something apart
Sing one for me
Sing one for you

Keep Singing when the lights go down
We'll make a record
It'll be swell
We'll make a damn fine record
Sing one for Sherrise Iverson's daddy
who was too busy gambling
to make sure she was okay
Casinos are made, of course, for little children
Sing one for those anti-homosexual assholes
who just had to come to Shepard's funeral
to send him off in their own empathetic style
They fuck my heart still
They fuck my heart so bad I can't ever ask them back
We all make such a damn fine sound
Sherrise Iverson and Matthew Shepard give us our
sheet music
Sing my friend and
sing like you've never sung one before
You got one damn wonderful voice

10/16/98

your love's wounded history

down the bad road
the only one left
i saw the stars hobble out
i recognized none of them
not their fault
the heat slaps you on the back
an old friend you figured you'd escaped
down the one bad road
where our fortune lived
your love's wounded history
became a subject for debate
they asked me to say a few words on your behalf
but the doctor warned me not to open my mouth
the stars still find a way to hobble out
when they die the news makes a big thing out of it
we on the other hand will never be stars
we will die and no one will make anything out of it
down that one last bad road
your shocks couldn't take the toll
you reach out to call triple a
no one answers
i recognized everyone that day
i tried to escape
they slapped me on the back
all of them old friends
i should have warned you about
down the bad road
where nobody pays
and everything goes

they still ask me to say something on your behalf
i open up to speak and dirt blows in
they could have built a better shelter
they could have prepared better food
soon evening will arrive
with a surgical team
and a smile

4/26/96

©*Mark Savage*

bus was crowded

the driver spoke all there was to know so fast
it spinned my head's hair
and hearing is not invulnerable
the world sputtered through the window
and sat in my lap, choking my
ability to see the future,
as if I really needed it or
wanted to.
the next stop is anywhere you
thought they would have you.
you reach into your deeper than
outer space pockets and
clumsily try to find the
address, perhaps on the dark
side of the sooner than not
moon, that will give you
a place to hang up your
mind and try to get some
necessary sleep.
The History of Nobody in Particular
is going to become a movie soon.
They are pouring a lot of hard to find dollars
into it.
When they come around looking to cast the
damn thing
i hope they don't forget how
I taught nobody to sing but me

2/1/98

In the house of the worldly weary

your heart jumped me late last night
i was trying to make it to the immune station
the one where once you're taken in
you never have to feel anything again
i almost got there
but your heart jumped me in the dark
tripped me up
i got found this morning
still vulnerable
the good music still swimming in my blood
asking me to take a seat in the great adventure
of the wounded bones
learning to escape the earth's gravity
in the house of the worldly weary
there is always room for another fool
struck dumb through love
nations dissolve
we rumble on
through it all
sometimes we don't even know our
own name
i gave my phone number to *a* dog
that needed a friend
the air
goes around and around
looking for a white sale
looking to land a bargain
all we can do is
bounce in it
toward the dancehall down the road
where our skin lives

6/7/96

Raw Alibi

all the good boys and girls
went off late last night in order to
disappear, if they ever get heard
from one of these days will you
send me a letter, will you build me
a tune, all good whiskey and the music
therein walked out early this morning
don't point a finger at me. i got me
a raw alibi, hanging out of both pockets,
hanging from each side of my mouth
the world ran off, leaving its kids and
husband and wife
don't ask me if i've seen it anywhere
i've been in traffic for years
and the film i came to see
burned up and nobody has
a copy

2/21/96

as bullets begin to ask us to dance

darting, can i call you darling? the country western
radio shot me in the right foot as i
wanted to come and tell you my story, in such
valedictory speeches they call the woman
darlin'. can i call you sweetheart
or some other noun of forgiving?
they told me about your bad days
how if you have too many of them in a row
your face swells and your heart
shrivels.
i can't guarantee anything i have stolen
along my journey to you
will ease your pain, but
maybe it won't add to it either
my hands are empty but willing to
hold up any end you throw my way
my heart is too full with your
fever, if i don't lash out
at something soon i will
go deaf.
My History of Being Nobody in Particular
is disingenuous in its learning to
be somebody too much of one particular.
my crowded bus derailed inside the dancing
policeman's station and
your address clumsily fell out of the
sky that has no mind
but one

it landed on my inadequate shoulders
and helped me to deflect the
bullets of not giving a damn
about anyone or anything
it might be easy to dive head first into
quicksand
it might be easy to disappear
even if your body is
there for the viewing
The oxygen here is getting a little better
each time i open my mouth to
ask it to dance
The doctor not only speaks your name
he writes love poems to all his
patients, even if they cannot read

2/1/98

Michael Lally

Sojourn

Your footprints in the dirt have written me enough
songs, I hope, to get me through this strange
upcoming weather. I would one day maybe find you
and put you in my arms, the arms that cannot begin to
hold up much of anything, without some kind of
sustenance. Sustenance has been kicked around
by very unreliable elements, and the Earth has seen
some torn up days lately. One day you disappeared
and nobody intelligent can say where you've gone to
hide. I might have said something easier before you
left, I might have meant to say something easier. Love
paraded by yesterday, in chains. They took it to the
penitentiary for telling too many lies. You can't tell
enough lies, sometimes. You were going out to take
part in a sojourn, you said, or maybe I just thought
you said it. I look up the word sojourn in the dictionary
and the light is hard to read by. I should have listened
to you when i had the chance. I should of learned
those dances you wore so important around your
heart. I'm a slow learner, I guess, but I'm waltzing in
the dark now all alone while the eerie music keeps
pace. I'm going to somehow learn to hold up my end
of things waiting for your sojourn to come to an end,
waiting for you to back up and fill those footsteps in
the dirt that talk to me when I want to desperately
learn again how to sleep. I always thought I could sing
good enough to survive. I always thought too much
while the music around me broke into pieces with no
home or future.

I Was Either Going To Eat Dinner Or Kill Someone

I wanted to either kill everyone
or eat dinner
I really didn't have time to
           kill everyone
so I ate dinner
 I suppose if we had enough time
       to kill everyone
we wouldn't eat so much
            dinner
we'd lose weight
anybody left alive we
            hadn't yet killed
would not call us fat
but I only had enough time
            to eat dinner
so I didn't kill anyone
and ate way too much

1/15/94

Buffalo

extinct hearts
hanging their flag above the good time
pole there in the soul of day
wish you could play a musical instrument
or aim that gun better
a song and dance this country
used to truly be
it says so on the matchbook cover
at the last cash register before
clearing out of town
going to go west and slaughter those buffalo
the idiot kid says in the parking lot of
hope
hey kid, you've gone west and beyond
nothing out there now but deep space
and mediocre food
he smiles, takes my hand
wouldn't really kill those buffalo
they smiled at me once in another life
hell, I tell him, washing the windshield of his car
in my other life nobody smiled at me
except the hangman
yes my true love can bake a cherry pie
the birds sing
as they slowly fly by
on their way to a sale
and then some

did your continent run out of heart?
we cans are almost empty
and the radiation isn't lying
wouldn't really kill those buffalo
it all takes my hands
leads me to the promised land
the one just up around that everloving bend
do people care about on another any less in 1997
than they
didn't in 1887?
i turn around, a mist begins to
recede. the dinner gong rings.
all ashore that are going...
the radiation never lies
he takes my hand, tells me a witty enough story
that I really don't get
but not wanting to seem any more stupid
than i truly am
i nod in agreement
as the sun disappears
without leaving
a forward address

10/27/97

in the central heating of the that's how it is beast

in the central heating of the
that's how it is
beast
the marriage ceremony is talking fast and backwards
the high wire act is on fire
the guys with the weapons of love
are shooting themselves in ail the foots they can find
even their own
when the world gets better
when the world wears a dress

S.A. Griffin

when the world walks into you at an all nighter
and puts its hands on your shoulders
looks you cold in the eye
and says I must have been crazy to ever walk
away from a wonder like you
then
and only then
will the fog get up and leave
you in the center of the impending
in the beginning of they hey now
with the rockets swaying
with the chorus line on their backsides
legs kicking in tandem against the hallowed sky
oh well
some days you think you got it figured
some days you shouldn't bother
in between is where we all wind up alive
in between is where we go hide
and the ceremony of wind
kicking at our heels
is the ceremony we trust
it blows us to the light
it blows us to the sun
it blows us toward the resonant
soft drink could be
it blows us oh so fond

10/10/91

The Shoot

Unmitigated landing modules of sway in the Hollywood
caffeine connective, my hearties. Eight days on
the Robert Vlharo hallelujah juxtaposition, and still
standing in languages not yet born. Welcome to my
movie debut and the words are waters we weave our
wandering across. Lock it up Carmine, in my head still,
as if just a second or so ago. Lock it up, we're rolling,
quiet in the house. Shut up. Actors just garrulously
babble on and on and on. Told Robert I was no actor
and did not want to have to memorize any lines. Was
told okay. I swung aboard the ship and spent eight
days on a new sea. The ditties there go something like
this

Dreamers and Desperadoes is this organic album and
the tracks within are full of everyone and the music is
the skin learning a new trade under some accessible
new sun. Don Blakely the singing man, I recognized
him as being in one of the great movies of recent
years, the neglected Short Eyes directed by Robert M.
Young, Albert Paulsen, who debuted in John Frankenheimer's
All Fall Down and then appeared in The
Manchurian Candidate. Yes, I gave him the little
pieces of paper. Write write write. Sing sing sing.
Rained a bit the first day out but then dear skies came
out for the soiree. Marco and Marcello, the twins,
made Espresso. Coffee coffee coffee. Americo asked
me to write a poem for Savannah Smith and then sign
his name to it. i said you best rewrite it in your own
penmanship. I am no actor, but I can mangle a tune
pretty well.

John Fiorito and myself rapped black and white real
movies, did John Garfield pirouettes, I sang John
prine's the late John garfield blues and here we go on
the merry go round of love and dreams. Gambones,
business reps, somebody run down to Micelli's and get
Stanton... I need Stanton for this shot... Micelli's
is closed. Turns out he was at Musso and Frank's.
Roll film. Roll illegal Columbia. Roll down your skin's
youth. The structure was there, I had no fear, the
actors seemed to wonder at first about the seemingly
chaotic undertones, but five days into the thing I could
see that Robert was conducting an opera, and we
were musical instruments to carry forth the tone's
tune.

Anne Helm drew a caricature of me, which
inadvertently got tossed. She did another one for me.
She asked in it if I was a desperado or dreamer. Both,
hopefully. The music swells. The music lowers. Jimmy
Di calls me the poet man. I call him the actor man. I
sing Prine's Donald and Lydia in one sequence. On
day eight, the final day, Savannah and Mihai cave in
and fall asleep. Phil shuts the door to the room they
are in. He hangs up a sign that says Do not Disturb. I
add, Humans Hibernating.

The lovely Kerry McLean picked me up every morning, got me to the shoot in time, and took me home. Actors looking for their next gig. Wouldn't realty want to be there. My day job called me home. Christmas season impending. Batten down the hatch, put the cat out, order up a salvo. Excuse me, do you work here? Write write write... Images dance out of images. The cats are out in the back, it is Thanksgiving, the food was plentiful and good. Don't rush. Instead of Action from now on I say Have Fun. Good morning is Buon Giorno, says Paolo Strozzi. He flew back to Buffalo with Joey Giambra and Charlie who worked with S.A. in Kessler's Las Vegas Vacation. The dancing sky got a working telephone. The dancing sky got no reason to cry. We do what we have to, we do what we can. The skin of the moment is growing a new forest. The new forest just wrote a hit book. They will make a movie of it soon, before we wake up. Good night. Dream well. I am both a Dreamer, and hopefully, a Desperado. See you soon on the new boulevard of upcoming and upthrust. humans, rev your potential and see you on the other side.

I have seen the Future and it is three days Stale

Yesterday I saw the Future
pushing your kid around in the school playground
while authorities looked the other way
and took money in the side pocket
The Future didn't like the way your kid looked
or dressed or spoke
The Future was glowing with vanity and
claimed it had the law behind it
Your kid was no match
I stood on the other side of the fence
watching the Future make minced ham out of your kid
I might have tried to defend him
but I never was big on causes
And the Future is very mean and ugly
and has a lot of influential friends in government
I sort of looked the other way and walked on toward
the
corner

Believe me
I have nothing against you or your kid
I'm just not the kind of hero
that tries to stand up to the future
now
if it had been the past
well
the past is kind of weak these days
it really doesn't have a lot of friends
influential or otherwise
I saw the past on a talk show once
it looked kind of anemic and done in
it handled the questions put to it by the host
very badly
your kid might have had a chance
if it had been the past
but the past actually liked your kid better
didn't care how he dressed or talked or thought
well
you can't buck the future they say
the promised land is up ahead
you just need to know the right people
to get in

11/24/94

Nomads of Oblivion *LRB # 25 – 2000*

Introduction

Inside of these pages you will experience the heart laid bare for the willing mind to undress in the flying museum of the word set free. In this revolutionary brave new world of technology

– ethics and emotions go on strike for better working conditions. Scott Wannberg writes poetry to liberate the overworked and underpaid. Love runs for president. The gods surrender and the muses are ecstatic. Finally, there is light. Scott's poetry holds you willing hostage in the present and disconnects the future. He writes the music: this book is the instrument and you are the conductor. Ride this train, it will take you home. Anyone can ride that has the ability to be available at the dance. Upon disembarking, give someone, anyone your ticket so that they may take the journey as well. That is the point. Give. The person who wrote this book is a giver. Good poetry is unconditional, and Scott's is some of the best. It is elemental like a song and this man's music will never let you down. The poetry in this collection is large and small like rain and wind. It will brand you in its blazing branches as it remains firmly rooted in the rich afterlife of the timeless season of someone who rides a soul bound by experience, insight and wisdom coupled with the ability to work his humanity without apology.

S.A. Griffin
June 21, 2000
Los Angeles

Border of Boredom

The phone coughed up blood when it heard you speak
The militia can't find the aliens in your soul
Some lonely patient swears by your cold
I wanted to go skating but the world was too huge
I sit in coffee some months beyond, some tones old
Rattle the illegal bones, shake up the orbit and grin
The takers and the took, they all love to sing
The cut up, the pristine, they all share the taxi ride
A howling season climbs aboard the ear
Take me sailing, take me whole
Come along and say your sooth
Ebb and flow, debutantes and vermouth, traffic is
opening its heart to allow us to glow
The border of boredom is on fire
The international house of pain is having
a closeout sale
The country is in my underwear
The universe you claim is in the way you roll
Christ, baby, I could get behind you
if the universe you ride
would learn to dance just
a little bit slow

7/7/99

wunderkind moon hallelujah

                             get in touch with my stumble
teach me the trade
       the crossfire of Jehovah
the landing lights should maybe behave
all arguments know where we live
             the banks are on fire the graveyard shift
wants better hours
get alongside my wounded shadow
       teach me the lingo
wunderkind moon hallelujah
rolling across the lawn
weapons cannot forgive or forget us
check out my new dance
it will call you out pretty quick
       climb inside my benevolent hearse
the parade is just beginning
       death is acoustic
            you won't even need words
when the recital lands on your skull

7/7/99

sweat river

five and dime you to death, they will
turn the fan a little bit southwest
Cro-Magnon Cerebral Cathedral invites you to drop in and
sway
the hours nip and tuck, the hours demand we say grace
a whole new moon rising over the shoulder of sweat river
where we come to find out just who we are in the end
game of things
a man who claims i am lovable
takes aim
a man who says he knows Jesus personally
tells me to come back much later
when the wolves are asleep and the
food might treat your insides better
where we come to find out who wrote the book that is us
the one book we never finish
just when we figure out that maybe its the last chapter
and all the characters have gotten their due
a new dance invades the wary blood
a new dance takes over
lightning and thunder soiree across the hemline of
sweat river
dream easy, the border guard says, tipping his hat
in our direction
we both know his gun is loaded
we both know his gun can fly

7/7/99

When the Laughter

When the Laughter called me up I was
somewhere looking for a way to behave
The odds on surviving got tall and
somebody came across the front of my TV
as if he knew me and began to
sing about all sorts of accommodations
that could be had for free if I dialed
the right 800 number within fifteen
minutes but the holes in the carpet
were growing large and the band was
running late, it gets that way at times,
I was looking for a way to tell time
without having to worry if it was actually
playing me straight, I was wondering
where the clowns had all gone,
I kept rummaging through
the closet and newer civilizations,
alive on
the other side of the wall waited for
laughter to call collect and let them
in on the punch line, oh, I heard
the line punched through by tired
men and women, the line was waving there
in the impending storm, I crawled out
of myself and began running across
the new bewildering highway. Somewhere
the light will hold, somewhere the
season will swing, come and join in
with some kind of heartfelt unison
as the cold climbs through your blood
and begins to sing, as the cold
washes your soul and begins to
sing

12/23/94

god didn't

god didn't make you kill that nation
you made god say he did but god
is just another woman standing in
some rain you can't predict and
you made up all those stories you
swore created the way the world
kills itself all the time
      god didn't put the ammunition in
your bones as you walked across thousands
of people who didn't speak your language
or dress according to your code
    your ego just keeps on pumping
at the vacant gas station of fools
   god did not get into your car
as you ran over anybody who got in your way
so when you tell me this on the tv with
your hands all knotted up with blood
all i can do is pull the plug out from the wall
and shake my remaining hairs out
in bewilderment
  you claim you know god personally but
i've been to his or her hotel room and
i didn't see you there
    the next time you raise the blade
and cut off the head of some poor hapless fool
that you don't like
  just don't bullshit me anymore
come out and tell me the truth
you just like cutting off the heads of all
the poor hapless fools you don't like
you're just a damn bully and can
get away with it until some bigger bully
comes and cuts off your head
that's the way it goes
here in the amusement park of
morons masquerading as
brains

3/8/96

Zapata is a White Horse

Maria dreams of a white horse
feeding off her blood
Agrarian skin will transcend
whatever government in Mexico City
currently struts a peacock feather
Emiliano is my white horse
the soil says as the villagers
go out to battle it and learn from it
or maybe for once get the upper hand
but God is not a Yaqui Indian
a wise man is quoted as saying
before gagging on too much
while down here in the village of
nameless men and women
trying to find a voice
whatever that might become
Emiliano is a White Horse
galloping across the
tired brain of the country
while in Mexico City nobody gives a damn
the city people read books and talk
philosophy but deep down
they give no damn

and when Zapata was gunned down
Maria said a rosary
and God came to her side
and ran his hand through her hair
and kissed her
while the fever sang
while the mad men ran over the world
and keep running over the world
and are running the world over
as we sleep dreaming of
Emiliano the White Horse
Even the myths grow tired
if not fed
Even the love grows hateful
if not
nurtured

1/29/95

In the House of Original Sin

In the House of Original Sin
everybody is a winner
although the plot is kind of
hazy and hard to figure
if God created everything in the beginning
then he or she created Satan or the Devil
and yet according to the director of
the movie God (he or she or it) gets
mad every now and then for the weakness
in us paltry humans, he or she gets
angry for humans falling prey to the
wicked ways and means of this aforementioned
Satan or Devil fellow (or woman)
but if indeed God created everything
and that means he or she created Satan
then I guess it eventually means he
takes it out on the pale humans for
supposedly giving in to one of
God's own creations...and if God
created not only Satan but the paltry
humans who piss God off by playing
in Satan's sandlot, well, I guess
God is just a schizo like all of us
and doesn't figure he is taking it
out on us for playing some of the
tunes God put on the jukebox in
the first place...and don't give
me that specious junk about it all being
some kind of a test, because if God created
everything, which some of those movies claim,
there is no reason to keep making up odd

spur of the moment quizzes, everything is
preordained and set up and all the graduate
committees are in place and the dictionaries
are all written up without any possible room
for adding on new words or visions or thoughts
so once again in the House of Original Sin
I guess everybody is a winner because if
God created everything, which the academy
award winning screenwriter says, then
he created the buxom woman who took the
bite out of the apple that the serpent gave
her and God also created the serpent who
brought the damn apple...I have nothing
against apples, in fact they are good for
you on a diet, and I never really hung out
with serpents, except now and then the two
legged kind, but once again I think God
needs to see some kind of a shrink and get
a little focused, it's like a kid building
a house out of playing cards, then creating
matches with which to put this house on fire
and then this same kid invents a fire truck
and fire men and a whistle and he begins to
get red in the face blowing on the whistle and
screaming Help Help Fire Fire Fire
It's just too complicated sometimes for
a paltry weak human as myself to
deal with. In the House of Original
Sin everybody is a winner
Hallelujah

1/22/95

this song is for...

this song is for the idiot that lives in the
wisest fool that ever loved me
      this city takes off its clothes
and complains about the cold
while we believe in the miracles in
the eyes of lovers as they dance
across the wounded ground
we call home
    everyone needs a light that can work
well enough so they can see their way to
the country of darkness
    the moon is crawling into your bed
listen as it whispers your favorite
song
  holy is as holy wonders
    take me to the vulnerable hotel
where the furniture always fits your
mood
 i took my baby sashaying
   i took my honey wondering
there's a place up the road that just might
love us for free
  there's a party going on somewhere in
the last name of our dreams
 this song is for the way we bounce
ignorant but mirthful
 as the pain takes a back seat to
the hope that hopefully never finds the
time or inclination to die
  come on and laugh in a language that
wants to be your friend
  come on and sing in a country
that will always find room to let you in

3/8/96

chairman of the board
for frank sinatra

his phrasing built a navy
of lovers on deck
as the ears of Hoboken
tunefully grew
up from the ten cents a dance
the big band cloud
addressed the mundane skin
fever's melodic soft shoe
as the ears of Hoboken
rhythmically flew
fly me baby
fly me to all the moons
his ways with a song
made the Earth
climb aboard
the dance
fly me then
beyond all
those tunes
get me there
and then some
the ears of Hoboken
become summer wind
and the vowels of the world
fall in love with the consonants of
the sky
and the vowels in this world
learn to leap wildernesses
with those swinging consonants of
time

5/17/98

The Golden Book of Thankful Screams and other bedtime rumors

The MEDIA splattered my love
because it was bored, needed something
to not do; The news stations grabbed me
by the neck, wouldn't, couldn't
let go; The Media pulled down my
underwear, their cameras probed
my vitals, looking for something to
give their audience: (Let's look at that parked car
again...there's nobody around it...but let us suppose
somebody could be around it... we're being asked not to get
too close to the motel, the suspect could be watching
television and we do not want to give away any plan the Swat
Team might be planning...
etc. etc. absurdity infinity...)
The bad guy had taken a taxi to Las Vegas
Now if the media there had been forewarned
but a whole lot of people spend their afternoons there in
rooms without clocks or television sets...even if the Las
Vegas version of Eye Witless News had been privy to the bad
guy taking a cab all the way out to their fair town, well,
one wonders about the audience demographics...
The bad guy was one of those intensive eyed guys who
believes so called White guys created the universe
White Guys that is with the right religious pedigree...
He drove all the way from Washington State to Los Angeles to
make his story a Media Boogie...Couldn't the Media in
Washington State have sufficed to play his rhythm structure?
The Thankful Screams make love on my TV screen
The anchors examine the love process and the cameras go deep
I hang onto my skin I hang onto my foolish hair
All the channels go go go
I turn them but they turn me back again
Cars with nobody in them
Swat Teams trying to negotiate with a guy already on the
road in cabs
Pensive looking men sticking mikes into the mouths of

even more pensive looking cops spokespeople
The cop guy says I'm calling this conference to basically
tell you there is nothing new to report but in about a half
hour when I have nothing new to report I will call another
conference
Come running and bring the hook
Bring the gag
Where's the damn shoot out?
We postponed Jeopardy and Wheel for this one baby

News used to mean something going on we needed to find out
The probability or possibility that something may or may not
happen is not exactly news

Spending all day trying to make speculation sound
like real event
is tiring
and your bones begin to cringe and crumble
the air gets redundant
the music cranky

Come on baby, bring a vision in your thermos
Tall thankful screams grow in insane mulch
No one is sacred No one immune
No one knows the exact time
Come on baby, tell us a story
Make my tired drag ass body stand up and take notice

Come on, anchor folks
give me a big wet one
put it right on my lips
i'm ready to grovel
i'm ready to fly
Stick your camera right up my nightmare
We'll go bumping against the flames for free

8/12/99

Unstrung

The day collapses in a weird fluid shape at my feet
when the National Monument calling itself Ego
melts into some unstrung afternoon of paranoia and
attempted nausea. Lukewarm ideas of profoundly
glib people simmer on the one working stove
at the end of the canyon. A gullible furtive
jazz symphony scratches its vision in your skin
as the palace guard begins to investigate the
condition of its feet. I look for the UFO
that will sustain me. The hammer kisses the anvil. The anvil
writes a memoir. The blood, sweat, and tears
open up a chair of air conditioned nightmares
called stores and we buy and buy and buy our
way into the labyrinth that offers no penance
gives no hope and last but never least
never carries exact change.
My love affair makes the matchbook cover
rest stop. My love is a stupid old man with
a smart walking stick. Across the laughing river
where unstrung hospitals snap their balanced books
the temperature becomes a newer country
and the lost optimists living there
are going to be heard from soon enough
when the dreaming light comes on at the
end of this strange browbeaten day

Once I was a tender avenue
Once I was a rap sheet with promise
and now the sky is calling on you
and now the sky is writing you letters with
so many sad songs in the ink
Did you carry the load, did you carry the tone
to a place we call yes
Unstrung ladies ask their unstrung gentlemen to
take them dancing
as the rapids quiet down
and the raft we call civilization
begins to drift us toward
some rumor of morning.
When the dreaming light finally finds us
done in at the end of the hall
we can land intact
we can grab the emergency phone
And the unstrung love
will string us both up
in some kind of
integrity
in some velocity of
hello

7/19/98

Hymn for nameless children

And the dust laughed
And the crying animals said we love you
I know where your heart hurts
the wound is a civilization
that has no interpreter
You will allow me to put my ear down against the burn
i will trouble you very little when
i sing your elementary school's favorite
marching song to
the black holes collapsing
over my shoulder
And the train station was swallowed
by the smoke of the engine of the train
when it said I love you
in the hidden language of the new dawn
when children were butter on the end of
dangerous adult knives
and the lunch crowd would always be standing on line in some
hard to pronounce town
where death was so easily accepted
And animals cry in tandem while
their parole officers sleep in
because it is a holiday in their bloodstream
and the national monuments of fear
have melted in the new peace accords
of pain

Wander then
with a lost room in your eyes
when we reach the rendezvous of
skin and intent
there will be time for yelling
and shaking off the bewildered shoes
there will be dancing in the
deaf zone
we will become nouns
of trust
waters of dreams
Wander then head first
under the poor sun of
good mourning
Your blood is reckless with love
Your blood is the way we breathe

5/26/99

LOUD AGREEMENT

The burning armchair fits my aching future easy
as loud agreements on pogo sticks
make their presence a sure thing
on the boulevard of would be understanding;
A new joke showed up this morning
young as could forbiddingly be
it had the savvy, it held the counter
despite all odds
all across the wounded earth
rush hour claimed its children
the new joke ran its fingers through our hair
it really wasn't all that funny
it simply sounded good in its telling
as dedicated men and women
stood in line in the rain
to prove they knew what to bring home
for dinner
even though none of us were hungry
for some time
on that slippery backyard of
bewildered horseshoeing
and vital statistics
screaming constantly over all the network news shoes
at once
the loud agreements toss and turn
arm wrestle and guffaw
sometime soon i will take you sailing
but right now all the water has been declared
unfit
sometime soon i will ask you to love me
but right now the heart has been
declared an enemy of the state

7/31/99

Continent of Slaphappy Fools

Nobody fights past their prime
In my alley I see the wounded hospital
struggling to lift the trash can
The time for weapons is timeless
the eyeless stupid kid at the gate
claims and flails at me
with his mediocre hands of death.
I calmly sit him down on the next train
going to hell and part his hair
quietly
In the dawn that is coming
In the heat that is sure
I looked for my lovers, I looked for my friends
Rank Strangers melting in the wind
The Continent of Slaphappy Fools
grows another head
The oceans begin to hum
In the rage that is ever-present
In the language that is not believed
I looked for the escape route
I heard the wires cross
I looked for your eyes
I was told they worked here somewheres
Rank Strangers broken with awe
Disappearing slowly in the sun
The bodies are full of i.o.u.s
the bodies have landed mean

5/22/99

at the end of the world

at the end of the world there was maybe time for
dancing and love

they knew your name before you said hello

they could tell you from the way you placed your feet down
on that tired wondrous Earth

at the end of the world
there is music and time for eating
the kind of eating where you feel the food
going through
the kind of eating where you hear the food
talking to you

they knew your name before you said where have i come to?

What strange solemn room is this

sing then all the plans you wanted to have time to make
all the plans that got you cold
when it all fell through

at the end of the world they place a large wooden dance
floor
under your feet
the fiddler begins to work his magic
you take off your shirt
you take off your pants
the night air is soft and cool
at the end of the world there is maybe time for
dancing and love

so it will go
when they wake up the town
and the boys all learn to sing in tune
and the girls keep their sense of humor
so it might go
at the end of the world where they knew you
before you even speak

all the plans you wanted to impress everyone with
all the plans that nailed you slow
at the end of the world where the music picks you up
where the music takes you all the way down

so it might sometime go
when they waken the sky
when they reach up and pull on the moon
when they pull down that full moon and hand it to you
all you can do it bounce it

up and down
slow
across the hair of the earth
across the namebadge of the earth
across the sheetmusic of the earth
at the end of the world
where all night
love sits in a recording studio
singing your tune

5/2/88 // 11/7/99

had to know

the phones broke their promise
they always swore they'd work for us
had to know the result
tried to get through
static said its name everywhere
i didn't really need to know such things
the poets are insane, the government warned
metaphors suck anyhow
had to know the outcome of
the mystery
a car got sent for us
we didn't fit in it very well
the circus has enough room for us
they always swore they'd be there for
us
which one of us is the clown?
Who walks the high wire and gets home clean?
Had to know the name of the new game
came with every good intention
reached into my one carry on bag
seemed there was a hole in the bottom
a long enough way down to go
tried to angle in
got hooked by angelic bait
the long road home has no parole officer
come and whisper your home's real address
the tender sky goes in for the night
its mother has been yelling for days

4/15/98

Drive By Love

everywhere i stumble
the hate grabs at my ear
i don't need any of it
where did the earth disappear?
Sometime late last night
it took off
without a change of address
i woke up trying to sing the good fight
i wanted to leapfrog rainbows
every motel these days is boarded up tight
nobody wants to join in the chorus
keep the pedal pushed to the floor
the next world up ahead just might be the one
you need
keep yourself vulnerable
keep yourself awake
they got a bullet with your name on it
i saw one last night
it looked so glib
it smiled so sad
we'll all get saved pretty quick
i read the future in a bubble gum wrapper
the future had clean fangs
love still held a door open
not in this century
but around the bend
love still had some energy left
bloodied and torn up some
it kept coming back
we'll get there soon hopefully
before the solstice

i stand at the edge of a fairly deep hole in the ground
but frankly it's not deep enough for me
to jump in
so watch me bypass it
give me time
there's a fever working here
trying to reach some apex of sweat
the heart is a mystery
you don't ever really want to solve

7/23/95

Richard Marcus

in this house of song all languages can stay up past their bedtime

                the new song got talked to late last night on my
new super hip get with it cable station
          the new song and its entourage were seen
skateboarding above oblivion
              the suave talk show host seemed to really be in the
know when it came to the metaphors of the new song
   he seemed uncannily erudite
then again it could have been the sound on my tv
it hasn't been working too succinct lately
  the new song hadn't been around in awhile
the host asked how things were going
 the new song got up with a sigh
and began to show the scars to the audience
the audience oohed, ahhed, clapped
   they cut to a commercial
i'd already bought more stuff than i needed that week
i ran away from the commercial
   i ran and got my copy of the new song's most recent book
for weeks it had shattered the nerves of
the reading public
   i turned to a page somewhere in the middle
and the music jumped into my sk
and took me sailing
   when it does that
      you never have to explain a damn thing
and the air is some country
   you can remember re entering with fondness
as the war around us all
just goes on and on
with nothing much new to say
    the talk show showed up again
the new song was dancing across my tv screen
it danced so very good
it danced so good i trembled

    i needed to share this
i opened my door wide
and outside all these new songs
were bouncing up and down
and nobody had to atone for anything
much
and nobody had to get anywhere too fast
for no particular reason
    new song ran for president
new song invented real love
    go on
let that new song walk up to you
let it jump into your arms
and call you home
    with a little over a minute left in the game
with the sky not groaning from taking on too much
    your feet tell your heart this simple
story
  anything is possible
and the dogs of war
need to take a bath now and then
    the new songs grab those proverbial smelling
dogs and
shake them up so hard
    the dinner is frankly
      on them

9/23/1996

jazz, your blood line

go dancing in the tired sky
love searing your skin
the news from the heart of the earth
sings a gentle frustrated yearning

call me when you finally land
call me when you need to cry

you go dancing in the lost and found
you go crazy in the please maintain shed

hard to know the right time to fold
hard to know when to soar

the law of gravity is cruel at times
the laws of men are strange and arbitrary

you ache for something tall
you long for coolness

ease this headache soft
dreams need not flinch in the path of
the barrage

jazz, your blood line

i've seen the results of your tests

we stand through the long and never short of it
we stand and hear the sound

the fear is only momentary

pick your tune well

the season is getting underway

rumors of love tap their vital code

along the woodland of your spine

didn't you even
ever wonder

i too collect fine tuned dust

sway with me in some
hapless tandem

name this world of a day

it's lit
large enough for the both of us

jazz, our blood
and all the nights and days
that follow

we are children out on parole
we are adults who have left our passports
and checkbooks back in something
calling itself civilization

unfocused, unfettered
ungoverned, unkempt
here we go
naming the impossible
and by doing so
making all discordance
somehow hummable
and perplexingly wondrous

3/24/87 // 11/7/99

the earth made of cardboard

the earth, created in cardboard
hurdles its hurt rhythm section
against the walls of the unhearing and
dances are not on time as the
skin of the city needs a way to let loose
the face of the city needs to learn seeing
nameless stairs of bones that we must dream our bodies
out from
lead the foot to a ritual of flesh
the one two three of it all the ways of the sky
climbing down into the open wounded mouths of
the nameless musicians of the street as the
ears of the hours of the molecules of the language
in the sky begin to weave tapestries of noise
speech becomes a way of wandering
along the bodies of the noon along the
children of the without
the raging quiet of love signals an upcoming turn
our bodies become tones that even animals cannot hear
and now the quiet days of seconds
driving the foot down onto the wherewithal of
the lexicon of the snagged sidewalk
you can bring the big theater downtown sonny
you can build the new tall edifices of the future
but where oh where will you park the cardboard box
suite now that Another Planet is gone to another
planet; name this dance hopeful, name this cartoon
human...we begin merging with each other in the
hurt mezzanine of it all, the calling out for
a witness, a recognition, a music, an empathy then
raise your fingers to the sun, any sun, for warm is
a continent after all locked up in the den with the good
china...can i get a witness? Can i get an amen?

The bloodstream says
yes
the heart against the corner of nothing much doing and
anything is possible
begin to breathe
the dance continues...

2/14/90   valentine's day

*The Carma Bums 1992,
Scott Wannberg with
Lorraine Perrotta,
photo by S.A. Griffin*

names in the paper

   stroke slow your old tooth of fear
     aim it under the pillow
   the drunk fairy is coming
     estimated time of arrival
   announced on the late night news
      keep your window open
   someone as dumb as me is coming
      if it isn't the good fairy or count 110racula
   or some minor thief
     a psycho or a guy hawking newsweeks
   it just might even be me
     what's left of me
   you pride yourself that your heart is immune
     i'm going to leap your city's teeth and burn it up
   they just let me out of night school head first
     my legs are dumb with the street
   keep that window open
     i've got dark beer jazz records stale pretzels
   i'm coming slow but i'm moving true
     there are cops nervous enough to stop me
   but they haven't showed
     i hear my friends got lucky
       some got aboard the titanic just in time to go down
         they got their names in the paper

new day in an old set of clothing

the state of the nation
got evicted last night
while we supposedly slept
but my bed doesn't vote just for anyone
i heard the state of the nation
in my yard
burrowing deep looking for that bone
that would keep it happy
it never got there
it still dug
when i ran out into the traffic
to find you and
tell you a story
that would keep you from
hurting yourself
the state of the nation
couldn't make the rent
they were going to make a glib movie about it
but that's been canceled
no doubt it will come to your house soon
to keep looking for love
i hope your siding
can take it

9/20/96

Headlights In The Sun

The dead men and women are throwing a loud large party for
us
The dress is emphatically informal
Soon the news will find us
Disheveled by misuse
Temperature gauges break down
before their best moments
Headlights in the sun try to find us
but the drinks are too endearing
Litmus tests fail miserably and their
results are yanked off the shelves of
esoteric bookstores all across the land
Hold yourself responsible as the wheel turns
Hold yourself intact as the preamble to a constitution
nobody ever asked for begins to unroll at your feet
Hold onto the love just a few seconds more
Hold on

7/19/98

she wore

she wore a mood
that opened the front door
of the war

she punched out her heart
in a long hall
made of light

her mind
sore from holding on
too long

the sea once lived in her heart

all the girls that drowned
there
became free
all the girls that sing there
teach her to
see

the sea once swam in her heart

she wore a mood that
kissed the backyard of the war

in a long hall made of light
air and fire marry

all the children that arrive
come first class
and never bleed

reworked and focused 11/6/99

Slam Dancers from Hell

your father sleeps with his loaded rifle
your father is a romantic man
your mother likes the way i stand close to her
at the kitchen sink

your mother never photographs well
last night we slam danced on some soft spoken floor
last night we hung each other out
your father talks to constellations when
sober
your mother used to navigate
tortured sounds
my parents aren't any less dramatic
my father sold defective guns to God
my mother invented the Migraine
she was always interested
in creating

3/24/87 // 11/7/99

Saturday

afternoon yells in its blood
suitcases alarmed, somewhat drunk
hear the train talking shit
across the forehead of known fields
soon summer takes you down
soon summer passes through your clothes
no rules to any of this
no guarantees
calmly assure no one
but yourself
you will be safely tucked in the bed of the world
by five a.m.
i begin to wonder
drollness rears its rhythm
Saturday evening stuck in its throat
calls us by name, height, color of hair, color of eyes
calls us by the lack of self confidence
we take with us
wherever we aim to wander
the ducks in the paranoia park
lately
are full of glitter
as they form new cities across submerged lakes
damn if you do
damn if you twiceover don't
doctor bills come, go
humming tunes written by a troubadour named
Michelangelo
a limit to the fish you can wear in your hair

in this zone
We reach Nogales, you begin to pull out your hair
Don't hurt me come Wednesday you say
I have to squint hard to see the calendar
must make sure
I know this seeming end of things
I know this end to things really never ends
Dancing schools are waiting on us in hell
the mind slipped through here some hours ago
Someone might need us to be total
Someone might want us intact
The time is on us
it rides in our blood
Flags of all subsidiary countries
wave their backbeat
as we roll by
Newly sung praises of holes in the heart of the world
soon summer nails our hope on some eerie wall of love
soon summer pares us to the essential ground
the smoke of good deeds rises from the middle named sky
the smoke of good deeds rises up to embrace the tune
these bleeding bones bend to bring

I do not know the end of things
Simone Weil starved herself to make people feel her
Drama School no doubt is colorful and wise
Amen to the hailstones that infect my vision
Pass the last fork because we are doomed to eat
something very soon today

11/6/99 reworked and rehummed

broken bat

in the coffee can sitting in the bathroom
a tiny person
who once knew all the talk show hosts
of hell by their first names
gives up everything
when his bat breaks
and in the days somewhat to come
we don't learn so much
language used to be compelling
a man who claims he is a doctor
shoves a needle into my right leg
begins to talk to me about basketball and murder
as if they had something to do with one another
did anybody claim ownership to the rain that began
to fall
when your bat breaks
everything else seems
redundant

7/20/86 // 12/10/95

Jesus walk

i don't like doing that Jesus walk
over quicksand

take your ever-loving swamp back
take back your poison snakes
just leave me my forty hour work week
show me a comfortable bed i can fall down on
if they blow up the planet, fuck em
i have nothing to lose but my poor idiot head
i don't want to do that Jesus walk over your quicksand
he frankly wouldn't make it either
everyone tries to say your name long enough
but my brain just isn't there to accept the going rate

reworked 11/6/99

About the Author
Scott Wannberg is related to Jimmy Hoffa's unknown hemisphere, and in conjunction with National Bone Structure month, has developed the significant 'No bones, no tell' diplomacy kit. Gondoliers have sung his unwritten thoughts in many different keys. His face is based on James Joyce's letters to Ward Bond.

Scott is also a fine human being who brings the light and smiles back to the party. He has a unique view of our world and he offers us yet another peek inside in this, his second Little Red Book.

*　*　*

Editor's note: in a rare twist of fate (in favor of the poet), **Nomads of Oblivion** *actually appeared, briefly, on the Top Ten List for Non-Fiction in the Los Angeles Times Book Review section in 2000 (I forget which month it was).*

from Eyes Like Mingus *LRB # 8 – 1999*

Ella – *August 1996*

ella fitzgerald sang
oxygen got discovered
the sun, on its way to the bank to the
bank to make a deposit
just sort of had to hang there a minute
bopping down and up to the tune
of ella's singing
ella fitzgerald sang
cities rose up from dirt
the buildings of them had people
inside them and
inside those people there were
stories and bloodstreams
that were the songs ella
fitzgerald sang
the sun really had to make it to the bank
before it closed
otherwise it would be overdrawn
and when the sun gets overdrawn
we all get burned
ella fitzgerald sang
armies threw down their guns
the time for dying
had not come to just yet
the sun hovered there
not wanting to go
ella fitzgerald sang
and the stories in her songs
are the stories that keep
us from going under

Special Edition Books

from Last Call: The Legacy of Charles Bukowsi – 2004

Bukowski Rap

Vulnerable heart driven acne
marked artist all too humanely
transcends myth. Films everywhere
at eleven.
Floated into Wildwood School
where the kids apparently
are private and not public, and read
poetry to two groups.
Both times when asked who influenced me on my so
called artistic gnarly road, one of the lights lit up on
Bukowski's name. No, I don't try to write the way he sang.
The late Bob Flanagan has a wonderful piece in his book,
The Kid Is The Man, all about the dangers of trying to sing in
Bukowski's key.
  No, I grope in my own lack of tune, but Bukowski opened the
unlocked doors. In the days when somewhat smaller, I guess I was

taught that poetry was an alien proper heightened attic room full of forms and manners and deft aerodynamic lingo that I, a paltry vernacular dullard, could not attempt to get, or have gotten into me.

Bukowski turned the light on that was already and always in each of us, but sometimes we have been taught we don't know where it is, or how it goes on.

You see, hear, feel, the way you see, hear, feel, and when you go to write it, you write it the way you might talk or see and hear and feel.

I've seen Bukowski Born Into This twice. It works both times. Didn't plan on going two days in a row, but the lady who wanted to go with me on Friday, went today, Saturday, and I met her at the theater.

Bukowski, beyond the babbling hyper PR myth(L.A. Booze Bard cracks me up, actually)is still Bukowski, storyteller of wounded backbeat.

As Richard Boone tells Paul Newman, in Hombre, mister you got some hard bark on you. Bukowski got some hard bark on him, and a lot of love, and a lot of pain, and a lot of fire, and a lot of love.

You cannot expect more from any artist.

William Packard got it. John Martin got it.

The hard bark that smiles above the vulnerable core.

The bluebird of the last piece read in the film, that bluebird soirees.

Rap me up, Hank. Roll me the highway. I hear you
          laughing. Crying. Singing.

THE COLORADO RIVER POEMS
March 2003

Gathering at the River

Late night early morning here we go
again S.A. and I
to this gathering at the ongoing process
of a Colorado River boundary between Nevada
and Arizona's lips…we stumble tired into
Harrah's where Ron has booked us rooms but
the desk kid is from Korea and stumbles over
too many words and thoughts…I keep telling
him how my name is spelled…can't find the rooms
listed under Ron…look under Wannberg…Paul Wannberg
he says they've all checked in…no, I say, I'm not with
them, they booked their own rooms…look under Ron
White, my stepdad…no listing…finally I have to wake up
Paul from solid sleep…they can't find us down here…
turns out the desk clerk had trouble when they came so
it got put under S.A.'s name…make room, get some sleep,
need to be down on the so called beach by nine thirty
for the scattering of the ashes…I ask S.A. to read
There is a River…Lorraine has to dictate it to him over the
phone the next morning…no rain this time…clear sailing…
stop at Denny's in Barstow…usually don't like Dennys…
turns out the steak and eggs are real and the waitress
has sense of humor…this trip shorter than last week as
its only twenty some odd miles from Needles to Laughlin
not too sure how the configurations all fit, California

Nevada Arizona we listen to John Prine on the way out
also Garcia and the Merl Sanders stuff from Berkeley
also S.A. brought Crime Jazz and Duke Ellington's Anatomy of
a Murder soundtrack…we stop on road and do some of Dennis'
herbals…don't want to smoke around the familia…find
that Bob and Danyl are only two rooms down from us
they go down without coming for us or calling…we all
meet on beach. I tell them S.A. is going to read. No problem
Eric is to do a prayer but when he does nobody can really
hear it, he does it so quiet…S.A. reads his piece I read mine
one I wrote the night before to commemorate this closure event
I call my mother oxygen and when her ashes start to hover
over the river they become oxygen…can't keep watching them
as the sun is right in our eyes…we take flowers onto the riverboat
thing and toss them into the river…Lynn has never gambled, being
a solid Mormon I guess, but she breaks her never having gambled
by playing in Mom's memory…We even have cold duck which
they call champagne which I guess is breaking another Mormon
no no…Ron's daughter Gail and her husband leave pretty much
after event…so does Ron. I guess we missed all the hanging out
the night before, coming in so late…S.A. and I both lose twenty bucks
at video poker…My brother Bob wins over a hundred dollars at
the slots…Everyone sort of disperses. I hug all the nieces and
nephews. Haven't seen most of them in years. I ask Eric if he still
writes poems. He says he's too busy making music. I say that's
poetry. Ron says before going, I miss her…I tell him you were good
for her…after marrying a lot of different guys, you were the
good one for her…Paul didn't get to Kingman in time last week so
part of him I am sure is torn up but he seems to be
holding okay…S.A. and I look at ludicrous ads for food
hanging in the elevators…We decide that in years to come
Laughlin will burst into a mini Vegas…The river purrs
along and gives it a tone Vegas never will get…My mother is
oxygen…Intake, out-breath…Rhythm, blues…The morning

drives its history into our bones…We bounce along as one
for a few minutes…then drift into tiny countries of
maybe we can hum it as one orchestra…
our tired yet hopeful biographies begin to
shimmer with the impending jazz
of a new afternoon that comfortably
lives inside your heart and can bounce up and down
to the ability of song
that struggles every day in
the skin tissue of yes…
yes, family of mine, this tired poet is pogo sticking it back
toward his imagination and what dances there
in the tired morning of what is your name and how do you
pronounce it and
is there a room for you on the planet
but my mom is oxygen
and without oxygen
you cannot stay at the party
so I breathe in deep and
say keep on partying

2/3/01

Colorado River Song

The singers live in how she danced to their rhythms
everyone needs to shake it loose
to repair, to rescue, whatever the rest of that quote says
the one by Doc Williams, one of my favorites
mom was a nurse for a long time
she helped repair, she helped rescue
songs live in how we hear their calling us
mom was, is a song
mom is a noun
nouns hold up the rest of the grammar
the colorado river doesn't ask questions
it dances here between Arizona and Nevada
the love of american indian cultures lived
in her skin, she hummed Kachina dolls and artwork
I could tell her things I wouldn't have bothered
trying to tell my old man
she helped me when I got tossed in jail with
Art Broughton in San Francisco
she paid my damn fine
I see her dancing on some beach
I see her dancing on all the beaches
and if there wasn't any
she'd make it happen
we'd drink brandy
I don't normally do the hard stuff on a regular basis
but we'd converse in brandy
once when I visited her in San Bernardino
even before she met Ron
she tried to hold back that her current husband
had split, after stealing from her
it came out, I sensed it, I wanted to know
the truth, she began to cry
I embraced her not as a son to a mother but
a concerned human for another human who's been

done wrong
needless to say I never saw that guy again
lucky for him maybe
mary danced, kept her heart open for
all possibility
Ron and her would drive from San Bernardino
to see my publication readings at Dutton's
today I am with my brothers and their families and
S.A. who once again got me here
to hear her singing as it
scatters in the moment of a river
and the nurturing that a river can do to
a land that needs empathy and sustenance
today my mother is oxygen
and the days ahead asking me to dance with them
in her legacy and rhythm
learn respiration, strength, vitality, empathy, texture and
love from
the love she sang

2/02/01

* * *

A Note About The Colorado River Songs
These two poems were published in a small chapbook as a special edition to honor the memory of Mary White, Scott's mother. It was conceived and executed by RD Armstrong as a gift for his friend.

Though not part of the Little Red Book Series, this short booklet used the same format, but with a different colored cover (green). It was never sold but was given away.

Now Scott is humming his own variation on this song, somewhere just beyond the horizon...just out of reach, but not out of memory.

RD Armstrong

About SCOTT WANNBERG

Michael Paul

SCOTT WANNBERG was a unique voice and a gifted writer, the gift being mostly for the rest of us, poets and friends of his. He was born in Santa Monica, California in 1953. A big man with an even bigger presence, he attended Venice High School and then went on to receive his Master's Degree in creative writing from San Francisco State in 1977. A "Carma Bum" from the beginning, Scott rode shotgun from 1989-2009. He was a poet's poet and a human's human who spent his life working as a sales clerk and book buyer for independent bookstores, most notably Dutton's Books in Brentwood, where he held court and worked the stacks for almost 25 years. His book, **Nomads of Oblivion**, made the *Los Angeles Times* bestseller list in 2000, and in the late 1990s, *Los Angeles Magazine* named him one of the "Top 100 Coolest People" in L.A. In August 2008, he relocated to Florence, Oregon, where he passed away too soon at the age of 58 in August 2011. Widely anthologized, his list of titles includes **Mr. Mumps, The Electric Yes Indeed!, Amnesia Hotel, Tomorrow Is Another Song** and **The Official Language of Yes**.

Bibliography

Mr. Mumps (Ouija Madness, 1982)

The Electric Yes Indeed! (Shelf Life Press, 1989)

Amnesia Motel (Dance of The Iguana, 1993)

Juice, The Musical! (Rose of Sharon Press, 1995)

Twisted Cadillac, with The Carma Bums (Sacred Beverage Press, 1996)

LUMMOX Journal (LUMMOX Press, 1996 - 2006)

Equal Opportunity Sledgehammer (LUMMOX Press, 1999)

Nomads of Oblivion (LUMMOX Press, 2000)

Harvey Keitel, Harvey Keitel, Harvey Keitel, with John Dorsey and S.A. Griffin (Rose of Sharon Press, 2005)

3 Fools For April, with Henry Mortensen and Viggo Mortensen (CD/DVD, Perceval Press, 2006)

Rockets Redglare, with David Smith (greenpandapress, 2007)

Strange Movie Full of Death (Perceval Press, 2009)

Tomorrow Is Another Song (Perceval Press, 2011)

All Your Misplaced Utopias (Bottle of Smoke, 2011)

The Official Language of Yes (Perceval Press, 2015)

The Man From Now (Rose of Sharon Press, 2015)

Harvey Korman, Harvey Korman, Harvey Korman, with John Dorsey and S.A.Griffin (Spartan Press, 2017)

Scott had over 750 poems published in numerous anthologies and periodicals.

Scott Wannberg: A Remembrance, An Appreciation

THE FIRST AND LASTING IMPRESSION you got of Scott Wannberg was one of hugeness. Of course his incredible physiognomy – this behemoth of a man stood at least 6'4' in his stocking feet, and surely weighed well over 400 lbs all of his adult life, looming over that cash register at Dutton's Brentwood, his only job title ever, that of bookstore clerk, mostly at Dutton's. He became iconic there, advising people what to read, his enthusiasm for the books he constantly read usually the guide. More important was the hugeness of his heart. He had a warm and tender love of living beings; cats and dogs, even human beings. His furry little friends made frequent appearances in his poems, nearly always as the vehicles of better common sense and decency than we have, or at least possessed of a kind of childish naiveté and wonderment at the madness and horrors of the world. He loved the animals. I remember long, long ago, in someone's backyard, Scott literally rolling around on the ground with a medium sized mutt named Elvis, and I remember remarking – "Look! Elvis is all dirty from rolling around in the dirt with Scott!" Commensurately, the gentle cats and dogs in the poems stood in for Scott himself. With fellow human beings, he was the very idea of kindness.

As gentle as he was, and he was consummately gentle, he was acutely aware of the pain and brutality in the world and these he rendered in his poems, gently but somehow with the requisite outrage. I guess you could say he had a huge social consciousness too. Which brings us to his poems, which were in quantity and quality, - you guessed it – huge. This guy didn't write poetry, he spewed it. In his near incessant verbal pyrotechnics and patter, were embedded, amid the torrent of words, neologisms, sparkling gems of all sorts, poems: intact poems. If for example a poem came to him, he'd feverishly run over to the typewriter (that's right, typewriter) and pound it out in a trice. It was always right, and blemishless – and oh yes, moving, thrilling, or sad, so sad. I do not believe the dude ever re-wrote a line in his life. And he may well have invented poems written for somebody about that somebody. As I said, at parties he'd rush to the typewriter, sometimes rushing back with this incalculably valuable object for somebody. He wrote 3 or 4 of those for/to me – exquisite, better than I deserve. Also, I am vastly proud to say that his very-popular-among-his-beloved-poems The Smiling Samurai was written in response to a poem of mine of a similar nature, and dedicated to me. Honor and treasure beyond price.

And the quality of his poetry was/is huge. Operating in a sort of improvised jazz sax solo analog, and it may be said, a wholly unique but sort of second generation Beat rap. He could read his poems from the rostrum, or he could rap it out ex tempore. His stuff is already seriously considered nationally. Shit, you know the one about poets becoming famous only after they Shuffle Off to Buffalo.

His verbal stream of consciousness could be bothersome if you were not up to it. I remember driving (I drove, Scott never did) to UCLA where we would be the twin featured readers. Piloting my little Chevette through evening weekend rush-hour traffic to Westwood was making me nuts, traffic always pisses me off, and the babble never stopped. It was then that I christened him "White Noise Wannberg" But is wasn't malicious, and he didn't mind, knowing it was affectionate. I loved him, and if you knew him, you'd love him. Everybody loved him. O, however special, he was human and had his quirks, but I'd be suspicious of anyone who didn't –uh -, love him, that is. .

One must mention his love and knowledge of movies. Guess what, they were huge! Maybe beyond huge here, encyclopedic hardly does it. I swear, he could tell you the third assistant cameraman in some nondescript '30s melodrama. He once confided in me that this body of information was the only thing he ever studied seriously. As he loved movies, so he saw them. He went to the movies with great frequency. I remember sitting behind him for some reason at a Santa Monica theater one night, - something in color involving Henry VIII and perhaps Katherine Hepburn, and seeing that most distinct hulking and now black silhouette – he looked very much Bob's Big Boy – thrown up toward the screen of whatever full color Dolby Sound wonder it was, and I remember marveling, Jesus this guy is where he belongs, in his element, in his glory, the king on his throne.

Scott and I had a love for singer-songwriter (the great) John Prine that bordered on veneration. Many were the John Prine concerts we went to together. One time, at the House of Blues, we sat on the floor, which was hard for me, and doubtless more uncomfortable for Scott. Didn't matter. It was Prine. In his last years of giving readings, Scott would sing a John Prine song, solo, alone, without the accompaniment of either other voices or any musical instruments. And Scott was no singer – though he steadily improved. This is a very ballsy thing to do, because it is even more naked-making than reading your own poetry in public. I can do it, not because I'm any ballsier than the next guy, but because I trained myself and practiced it, because as I said at his wake – it's "part of my act". So I sang Prine's immensely moving and funny "Please Don't Bury Me" – now so strangely and obliquely apposite. They scattered one third of his ashes on the lawn of Beyond Baroque. Scott filled 3 normal, uh, "cremains" containers.

When I first met and heard him, as we became friends (again as I said at his memorial, it was at Beyond Baroque – 3 buildings ago), I wrote him a poem to him about him. It was called The Voice of the Mountain. Scott reminded me of a mountain. In it I tried to incorporate the strange razzle dazzle prosody of love that was SW. I wrote another memento mori poem after he was gone. Book ends. Like many of us, Scott was born after I was, and died before I will. I, like so many of his older friends, we poets of the '70's, form parentheses around his life. This too, though sad and heartbreaking, may be the consummate gift, - that he lived at all.

Strange to behold that he lives on in the hearts of those who loved him, however much a cliché, however saccharine sounding, especially to those of us who practice the craft which tries to revivify language, is nonetheless true. This was a guy who was larger than life, who so powerfully affirmed life.

Steve Goldman— a poet, was a friend of Scott's from the early 70's onward.

I FIRST MET SCOTT through francEyE sometime in the 1980s. We would go to Scott's readings and then, I would drive them both home. Other times, the three of us would go to poetry readings together. They so valued each others work and friendship. His insights into poetry and the stories he shared were piercing and thought provoking. He introduced me, through these conversations and his poetry, to John Prine and other singer songwriters, a gift I am most grateful for. francEyE scheduled Scott to read his poetry at the Church in Ocean Park series. I will forever remember the cadence of his poetry and the music he incorporated. He also traveled with me to bring Joseph Hansen from Laguna once Joe had moved from LA, to read with francEyE and be on a Church in Ocean Park panel. What an amazing car ride!

It was a delight to join members of Carma Bums at poetry readings and at Father's and other clubs in L.A. What adventures they had inspiring us as they traveled throughout the states and brought back vivid descriptions of the people and places they toured.

Once I realized Scott was also a key person at Dutton's Bookstore where my good friends Ed Conklin and Cathy Cohen worked, I would buy books for the gemology library I work for as well as books for myself. Scott was always a fount of knowledge about these books as well as introducing me to new poets. His excitement and understanding helped so many of the patrons of Dutton's. I loved to talk to him about movies and sometimes we would catch the new John Sayles' movie or another independent film together. Once he moved to Oregon, I had his Facebook postings to connect me almost every day. There is a giant gap in my life with Scott gone. But, we have his books and a wealth of poems to treasure and pass on to a new generation.

Dona Mary Dirlam— friend and fan of poetry.

Scott Wannberg and the punk rock-bebop-Deadhead American dream

ANOTHER ELECTION GONE, and I'm thinking about Scott Wannberg. Scott Wannberg, dancing in his chair as the Clear plays at a *Blue Satellite* release party at Highland Grounds. Scott Wannberg and the Carma Bums at Upchurch-Brown Booksellers, making the audience forget the madcap band of poets made them wait an hour for the show to begin. Scott Wannberg in the *Los Angeles Times*, more famous as a bookstore clerk than he ever was as a poet.

I think of Scott, and I always picture him joyous, always dancing – in love with language, music, cinema. It was easy to be happy around Scott, when he came to the table you were sitting at and spontaneously wrote you a poem. It was easy to forget he got angry, too. This election would have made him angry. He despised violence, and cruelty. He had a hippie's disdain for war and a punk's intolerance for bullshit. In "my government broke its funny bone blues rag..." he wrote, "nobody wants a government. / they all are rock stars / with rocks in their heads / and no no no / is the astounding resounding yes yes ..."

Scott thought in poetry, one of very few people I've known who do that. There was a beat playing inside his head that no one else could hear. He saw the world in a series of interconnected metaphors and symbols. And for all his sweet spirit, he was neither naive nor stupid: Show him a demagogue and he would see all the pain and fear and anger for which that demagogue was a metaphor. He always wanted a song or poem that would heal those wounds, but I don't think he ever expected it to come. But still, people shake their fists at Trump's election, and threaten to leave for Canada or Europe, and all I can think of his Scott's poem, "The Dancer Steps Forward," where he wrote:

> *"The dancer stays home*
> *digging in his earth, looking for the bone that will*
> *sing to him.*
> *"His friends have run off to Europe.*
> *They groan, pull their hair, wail,*
> *America is a paltry place for the imagination.*
> *They hit the walls, deny their past.*
> *They become good Europeans."*

Scott never pretended he was anything he wasn't. He was a poet, and a bookstore clerk, and a lover of music, and he was an American. That meant a lot to him. In the end, he never flinched at the country's dalliances with darkness, although sometimes they angered him, in that way that only someone you love can anger you. He believed in freedom, more than just about anything. In his own punk rock-bebop-Deadhead way, he believed in the American dream, and he dreamed of America being better.

> *"There is a music in the American idiom,*
> *he says*
> *and wipes his face for the last time,*
> *and begins to think about going up to bed.*
> *Tomorrow is another song."*

Victor D. Infante— he's the editor of the online literary journal *Radius*.

Scott Wannberg in Florence, Oregon, July, 2010
-- Rev. 4-1-15

People who have long dropped out of sight are visible here.
Scott's the only poet in town;
Being Scott, he's secure on this spiderpoint of coast.
He is very large, but his
true presence is light.
Bright wings of morning
in the cage of the body

Off the main road, he pays low rent and lives
Next to a police sub-station he waves hello to.
I sleep on couch cushions hopscotch on the floor.
We talk the old stuff: SA's mac & cheese
Dutton's deceased bookstore, the endless forever Carma Bums,
How Dustin Hoffman leaped up when he heard
Scott was waiting for him with books! "What? Scott waiting for me?"
   Yes, Dustin jumped for Scott - and Mr. Dylan, Jackson Browne
   And all those movie people with the flagship names
   Always sought out Scott
Because he was already an angel,
and lifted them up
despite their weight of fame

Because he was a Colossus of Soul,
Flitting on heavy feet between the stacks
Finding first the books you want, then the ones he wants for you.

I remember the carbo-mad burgers and fries
At Early World eatery across the street in LA and
The recent year Scott couldn't sleep,
like he was stuck inside his own TV.

Time to eat! Ding dong!
Always a ceremony of delight,
The action is down at Thornton's family restaurant.

We walk there, Scott truckin' that oxygen tank
Behind him on its little mouse wheels.
Transparent breathing tubes corral his nose.

He takes 'em off once we're inside, oh yeah -
3 waitresses serve him 3 meals each sitting.
They fawn over him, Scott, of course they do!
We all can't help it. He's the consumate consumer.

I'm proudly here as "friend of Scott,"
That much-littler guy on the other side of the table,
visiting from that tormented giant LA Scott's from,
and these folks have only "heard of" ...imagine that!

It's so local here
I'm wearing a big white bib, too, like Scott,
Oh party down! Here comes the food!
Biscuits, pot roast, salad, mashed and those twin
Wedges of pie not long after.

To offset, post-lunch exercise striding with big Scott feet
10 times around the parking lot...
I thought he was doing well –
What a surprise this COPD he's got
Pulled some briny rip-cord in his lungs, even though
His weight's down and he talks like heat-lightning –

That's why I can't figure why he just blew off the personal skin,
And tears come out of me
Like spray from the boiling ocean only a mile away.

Our conversation veers on bat-wings between
corridors of books, expands
at the speed of light --

Towers, bungalows, apartment buildings, cities of words,
constellations congest slowly in twists of brilliant cosmic dust

In his apartment, we burrow into the stacked books.
I leave with an armload he's just ploughed over. We
Argue both sides of the 1846-48 Mexican War.
He says how some local kid he befriended
and even saved from suicide, ripped him off for several grand on a "loan" –
   No need to collect that now.
   And no need for suicide.
   God does it fine without our help.

Sure, the tombstone crowd is waiting in the wings,
And the virtual world is hungry for more lambs from Scotty pastures.
   But he's left me stark awake on my desert island of mortality
   His poetry marks my forehead like a track-meet of ancient bards,
   His spirit flashes by like a huge wedge of apple pie,
   streamers of ice cream flinging flavor;
   Desserts of Valhalla

That's after the rare steaks of love and
words you served up for so many years,
Scott, and your friendship,
More precious than an evening repast with any god
Or heaven I find in menu or holy book.

> ***Doug Knott***— actor, impromptu performer & attorney, served with Scott in the Carma Bums and hung out with him for 25 years or so.

The LUMMOX Press was established in 1993
and has published the Little Red Book series,
the *LUMMOX Journal,* and publishes chapbooks,
a perfect bound book series (the Respect series),
a Poetry Anthology & Poetry Contest (annually),
and "e-copies" of all its books.

The stated goal of the press and its publisher is to
elevate the bar for poetry, whilst bringing
the "word" to an international audience.
We are proud to offer this book
as part of that effort.

For more information and to see our
growing catalog of choices, please go to
www.lummoxpress.com/lc

www.ingramcontent.com/pod-product-compliance
Lightning Source LLC
Chambersburg PA
CBHW031630160426
43196CB00006B/355